Understanding Panic Attacks
and Overcoming Fear

Understanding Panic Attacks and Overcoming Fear

DR ROGER BAKER

A LION BOOK

Copyright © 1995 Roger Baker

The author asserts the moral right
to be identified as the author of this work

Published by
Lion Publishing plc
Sandy Lane West, Oxford, England
ISBN 0 7459 3313 0

First edition 1995
10 9 8 7 6 5 4 3 2

A catalogue record for this book is available
from the British Library

Printed and bound in Great Britain
by Cox & Wyman Ltd, Reading

Contents

Preface

My people are destroyed by lack of knowledge
HOSEA 4:6

In the whole area of emotional difficulties there is nowhere that the haunting phrase 'destroyed by lack of knowledge' applies more than in panic attacks. The lack of information and mistaken ideas surrounding panic are enormous and only increase confusion and fear in the unfortunate sufferers. Yet when I looked in bookshops all I could find was *Stress management and the business executive, Healthy body: healthy mind, Stress and healthy lifestyle*. All this was too vague, and mostly too unscientific, to be of much use. There seemed to be no one telling sufferers what panic was and what to do about it. What was needed, I thought, was a detailed look at panics that could help sufferers identify their baffling symptoms and bodily sensations.

I had had a good start in understanding panic attacks from the first day of setting foot in the Clinical Psychology Department at Aberdeen in 1977. Malcolm McFadyen, a senior psychologist who is even more Scottish than his name suggests, warmly welcomed me but almost instantly began to bombard me with his theories and observations about panic. He strongly influenced both myself and a whole generation of psychologists in the department with his 'Cognitive Invalidation' approach.

Most psychologists seem to have some pet obsession or other but the surprising thing about this was that hardly any mental health professional at that time had heard about panic attacks. Even in 1984, speaking at a clinical psychology refresher course in

Liverpool University Malcolm had to explain what panic attacks were, and there was scepticism from a few senior psychologists about whether such attacks existed or not! Much of this book builds on his insights.

After working for several years with panic sufferers I began to be dissatisfied with my understanding of panic. I wanted to understand more, root out mistaken ideas and clear my vision. I decided to ignore all my concepts about panic and start again at the drawing board. Actually, this is impossible to do—you can't break away completely from familiar patterns of thought—but as much as possible I wanted to be open-minded.

Where should I start? How could I be unbiased? I decided to start with the sufferers, from their point of view. Amassing as many autobiographies of panic and agoraphobic sufferers as possible, I immersed myself in them. I conducted a series of open-ended interviews with panic sufferers, tape-recording and transcribing their comments (most of the quotes from this book are taken from these). I gathered case histories. In therapy I tried to listen with a new ear, seeing if there was something important that had been missed. I also collected information on large numbers of panic sufferers, normal individuals and other patient groups using standard psychological questionnaires and statistical methods.

Throughout this process I have tried to get to grips with the nature of panic. *Understanding Panic Attacks and Overcoming Fear* has taken over five years to complete. I hope that in its pages panic sufferers will find some of the answers to their worrying and confusing experiences.

Roger Baker
2 January 1995

1

Panic: the Life-Changing Event

'I would gladly have sold my soul to the devil for just one day of complete health. I would unhesitatingly have given away everything I had to anyone who could have guaranteed just twenty-four hours of normal health.'

'I have been a sufferer for almost twenty-nine years, since I was serving with the Royal Navy. Of course I don't have to tell you the hell that I have existed in.'

'I see a man hobbling past my house on crutches, a cripple for life, and I actually envy him.'

What are these people talking about? Why are they so desperate? What is it that is so bad that they would envy a man on crutches? The answer is panic anxiety.

We all know what anxiety is like—before an exam, or when we have to give an important speech, reach the finals in a sports event or go to the dentist. But when anxiety breaks through into a person's life in a really powerful way and there seems to be no good reason for it, that is different. Daily life, work and relationships can get more and more disrupted by these unpleasant feelings that can't be controlled.

Like living in hell

It can really begin to feel like living in hell as sufferers twist and turn trying to shake off these feelings. People with panic anxiety often say that it is impossible for others to understand what they are going through, 'like explaining the colour red to a blind person'. The frustrating thing is that once they seemed to be leading an ordinary life. Suddenly, one day, panic struck, and everything changed. Now they live in dread of unbearable panic feelings and wonder if they will ever get back to normal again.

Mrs A. went to the checkout at Safeway to pay for some shopping and felt her heart starting to race and her mouth go dry. She couldn't get her money out of her purse because her hands were shaking so much. She rushed home. After this she was overcome with anxiety every time she left the house alone. She had to be accompanied by one of her family. Even now, years later, she dreads going out of the house, and goes to great lengths to make sure she is never left in the house by herself.

Miss M. loved her job as a travel consultant but, after a panic attack in a busy train in Italy, gave up work altogether, and after a long spell was only prepared to work in a rather undemanding job involving no travel.

Mr P. would start to shake and tremble and feel nauseous during meetings at his work in the oil industry. He was sure he would vomit or be seen shaking by his colleagues, and had made so many excuses for leaving meetings that he felt his job was in jeopardy.

Mrs C. dearly wanted children but because of panic attacks put it off and off until it was too late. 'I thought, "how could I cope with a baby? . . . so often you're housebound."'

These are descriptions of people who have had panic attacks. No two people describe it in quite the same way. For some it is the heart palpitations that are unbearable, for others dizzy sensations or feeling unreal, and for others difficulty in breathing or choking sensations. But they all share one thing. Their lives have been devastated by panic anxiety. One attack on a fateful day turned their life around and took it in a direction they did not want or choose. It made them look inwards at themselves rather than outwards. It put a strain on their relationships. It was a daily source of dread.

What is a panic attack?

Throughout the centuries people have suffered from panic attacks.

In sixteenth-century France they called them *terreur panique*. One English writer described panic attacks in 1603 as 'sudden foolish frights, without any certeine cause, which they call panique terrores'. Sigmund Freud was one of the first to give an accurate description of panic attacks in 1884, calling them 'anxiety attacks' rather than panic attacks. Panic attacks were fairly much ignored by the medical and psychological professions until a century later. In 1980, the American Psychiatric Association included 'panic attacks' in their *Diagnostic and Statistical Manual*, a sort of psychiatrist's Bible for diagnosing emotional problems. The definition in this manual has become the accepted standard of what a panic attack is. The updated manual of 1987[1] states that the following thirteen sensations are the main ones to occur in panic attacks:

▶ shortness of breath or smothering sensations

▶ dizziness, unsteadiness or faintness

▶ palpitations or heart rate speeding up

▶ trembling or shaking

▶ sweating

▶ choking

▶ feeling nauseaus or nervous tummy

▶ feeling unreal or 'depersonalized'

- numbness or tingling feelings
- hot flushes
- chest pain or discomfort
- fear of dying
- fear of going crazy or doing something uncontrolled.

To qualify as a panic attack, four of these feelings (any four) have to start suddenly, unexpectedly and become quite severe within a ten-minute period. There should be no obvious life-threatening situation setting them off.

Many sufferers experience more than four sensations. The sort of sensations they notice may not be exactly the same one week as another week. What bothers one person may not bother another. The term 'limited panic attacks' is used when someone suffers from only one or two of these feelings out of the blue. I'm saying 'only' one or two, but this gives the wrong impression, because for these people one or two of these sensations catching them unawares can be worrying, aggravating and frequent enough to spoil their lives.

Can I be normal if I have panic attacks?

Although the *Diagnostic and Statistical Manual* has been very useful in drawing attention to panic attacks, it has been unhelpful in another way. The manual invented the term 'panic *disorder*' for people who regularly have panic attacks or live in fear of panic. While it may be useful to have a medical-sounding name for insurance claims, it unfortunately gives the impression that the person is suffering from some sort of medical illness or disease, which panic is not.

Panic attacks can be completely explained by normal psychological processes occuring in a normal mind. They can be explained with reference to the unhealthy way people have learned to cope with life's stresses, their lack of knowledge and

12

misunderstanding of what is going on in their bodies and their *fear* of what might happen to them. Fear, lack of knowledge and misunderstanding are common to all humanity and have nothing to do with illness.

Can fear and panic be overcome?

Many sufferers have looked for help from different quarters. Some go to their own doctor and are helped by the drugs they have been prescribed. Some get referred on to specialist cardiologists or neurologists, believing that they are suffering from a physical disease, and are left confused when nothing is found. Others seek the advice of friends, go for counselling or to the clergy. Some find their way to short-term relief by using alcohol. Some scrape along—somehow coping but never living life to the full. For others nothing seems to work—it is like living in a nightmare.

But is it possible to change? Can the feelings disappear? Can life be normal again? The answer is, yes, it is possible to change—not overnight, but it is possible. This book is written to help people through the maze of panic symptoms and to emerge at the other side free from their domination. It is certainly not easy, and not quick, but it definitely is possible.

Who is this book written for?

It is written for three groups of people.

▶ It is a self-help guide for panic sufferers; this is its main purpose.

▶ It is intended to help relatives, partners and friends of panic sufferers to understand their problems and to provide informed help to the sufferer. Usually these people suffer too, because the problem is so baffling and they are never sure of the right way to react to the sufferer. Should they be firm, sympathetic or what? Is it illness, or weakness, or is the sufferer overreacting?

▶ It is also designed for therapists to use alongside their therapy sessions. For about four years now I have given clients early versions of Chapters 4 to 8 to read between sessions. It can help in backing up what the therapist has said. Clients often find that written material helps them in digesting the information and adds to the therapy.

Therapists vary greatly in the approach they take to problems. I have tried to bear this in mind—different therapists will find that different sections in the book complement their own approach. In this case they need direct their clients only to the sections that they feel are relevant.

Can people help themselves?

One of the worst problems about panic and anxiety is not knowing what is happening. I have called this book *Understanding Panic Attacks and Overcoming Fear* because I am convinced that understanding is one of the main keys to unlock recovery.

UNDERSTANDING

I have seen many clients in therapy whose panic attacks have faded after one session of explanation about what they really are and what they are not. Knowledge about what is happening to them brings reassurance and hope in place of bewilderment. Part I provides some basic information about panic. Part II explains what is actually happening during panic and deals with common misunderstandings.

Another important part of understanding is in a personal sense—why did this happen to me? Part III of this book is devoted to understanding causes of panic; it provides a seven-point programme for working out the links between events in the sufferer's life and panic attacks.

Part IV of the book describes a programme of practical therapy exercises to overcome the fear of panic. This is a psychological treatment programme that was originally devised by psychologist Malcolm McFadyen in the late 1970s and used at the Department of Clinical Psychology, Aberdeen, Scotland to treat hundreds of anxiety sufferers successfully. I worked closely with Malcolm McFadyen over the last 15 years in developing the approach[2]. The technical name for the approach is 'Cognitive Invalidation' and it is based on the theories of George Kelly[3]. It is similar to the Cognitive Therapy approach practised nowadays by many clinical psychologists, though it has different roots. It does not depend on the use of drugs, on relaxation, deep breathing or trying to change thought patterns by 'reprogramming'. Many sufferers find that if they know the right approach they can go ahead and make progress fast.

WITH A LITTLE HELP FROM MY FRIENDS
I would advise anyone intending to use Part IV of the book to have a friend or partner to back them up. The helper should also read the earlier parts of the book. This will help them to understand what the problem and the treatment are about, so that they can support and help the sufferer who may feel like giving up or become impatient with their lack of progress (this nearly always happens).

PROFESSIONAL HELP
Some sufferers, despite having a friend to support them, need a bit more professional help than this. They may need to contact a clinical psychologist, therapist or local self-help group to help them recover.

USE OF DRUGS
The therapy programme in this book does not depend on using medicines or drug prescriptions. It doesn't mean that sufferers should stop using any drugs they are prescribed, but that if they want, people using this book can overcome panic without drugs. Some people are against using drugs because they would prefer to be in control even though this involves some suffering. Others prefer to take something that may help to reduce their suffering.

This decision is completely up to sufferers. They should not feel guilty if taking drugs; on the other hand they should not feel that the *only* way to recover is through using drugs. It's a matter of personal preference.

Where do the ideas in this book come from?

The information and ideas in this book came from seven different sources:

▶ experience in treating panic attack sufferers over an eighteen-year period in the UK National Health Service and in private therapy

▶ reading research documents on panic and communicating with leading authorities as part of compiling a book called *Panic Disorder: Theory, Research and Therapy* published in 1989[4]

▶ study of autobiographies and published case histories on agoraphobia and panic[5]

▶ a research interview study carried out on twenty panic sufferers in 1990[6]. Interviews were tape recorded and transcribed. Most of the quotes in this book are taken from these interviews.

▶ the development in the theoretical understanding of panic at the Department of Psychology, Aberdeen from 1977 to 1994[2, 7]

▶ research information gathered on 130 panic and anxiety patients, 177 medically ill and 521 ordinary members of the public. Information was gathered on the last two groups to compare with panic sufferers[8].

▶ an evaluation study carried out on every patient seen for therapy at the Psychology Department, Aberdeen between 1991 and 1993, including every panic sufferer seen during that time[9].

The proof of the pudding is in the eating

There are many books and magazine articles on the general topic of stress and anxiety, though not much specifically on panic. Much of the advice given is not properly researched. Does the psychological treatment programme described in this book really work?

The study carried out in the Department of Psychology at Aberdeen from 1991 to 1993, assessing every patient seen for therapy, was used to test this out[9]. Every panic patient referred

Fig. 1: Panic attack sufferers; improvement during therapy
Average scores from 20 clients.

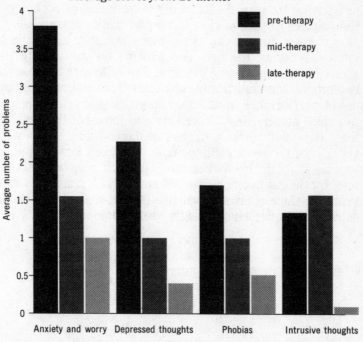

0 = average scores from the general population

to the Clinical Psychology Department for therapy by a GP or psychiatrist between 1991 and 1993 was assessed. Patients filled in a self-report questionnaire on their problems before they started therapy, three months after therapy had begun and after six months, which was towards the end of therapy. Other patients on the waiting list who had not yet received any therapy filled in the same questionnaire over six months to act as a comparison for the panic group in therapy.

Figure 1 (previous page) shows how much panic sufferers changed during the course of therapy. The figure shows how many problems/symptoms the patients reported before, during, and after therapy, divided into four main 'symptom areas'. The zero point is based on the scores of a large sample of local people; this helps us to see how close to 'normal' panic sufferers can get after therapy. As you can see, in every symptom area patients improved during therapy. The patients on the waiting list showed no change during this time. The difference between the two groups was statistically significant. This indicates that the use of the Cognitive Invalidation approach significantly helped to reduce anxiety, fear, depression and intrusive thoughts for these panic sufferers. By the end of therapy their scores were very close to scores from the sample of ordinary local people.

This suggests that the cognitive approach is successful when used by clinical psychologists. What this book aims to do is to make the same approach available to readers, and provide an extra resource to therapists as they treat panic sufferers.

PART I

The A to Z of Panic

2

Panic: When and Where

Panic attacks or anxiety attacks first occur 'out of the blue', suddenly, for no obvious reason. A person may have been living much as anyone else does with the usual stresses and strains of life when one day they experience a panic attack that is the start of a long period of misery and change. The peak time for first attacks is between the ages of fifteen and thirty, although attacks can occur at any age.

I have often asked people what they themselves call these attacks. Often they give it the name panic without having heard of it from anyone else. Some people think of it as a nervous breakdown—'I had a breakdown'—and they feel they cannot carry on at work or have the same active life. Sometimes people give up promising careers.

Out of a clear blue sky

The worrying thing about a first attack is that it comes without warning and sufferers can see no good reason why such a dramatic thing should happens to them, though, as I will show later, there is always a cause. What can really confuse people is that the first panic attack can strike when they least expect it—during a relaxing weekend or on holiday. They might understand it better if it struck whilst they were under a lot of stress at home or work, but not when it seems unconnected to stress.

After the first panic attack more attacks can happen over the next few days and weeks so that they become a regular feature of life.

There are seven common patterns of panic.

Place

Some people find panics occur in certain places, such as crowded shops, travelling in a bus, standing in a queue, in church, being down town. The name agoraphobia, from the Greek 'fear (*phobos*) of the marketplace (*agora*)', has been used in the past for this type of panic. For these people 'safety' is also a place, usually home, where they begin to feel secure and relieved. They may try to avoid crowds and shops, sometimes to the extent of becoming completely housebound. Here are a few examples.

'It was a Sunday. I went into the Bingo and I couldna concentrate. My hands started shaking. I tried to mark the number off the card. I couldna do it and I telt misel—"dinna be sae stupid". I couldna see the number you know. And my hands started shakin and I felt ma body ... yer stomach was rumbling ... and my neck started to twitch and I says me, "I'm nae going back to Bingo" cause I felt some people was looking at me.' ANN P.

'I began to have attacks in crowded places—particularly the student union at weekends. The predominant feeling then was that I could not breathe, although my heart would also be racing. When this happen I would generally leave and find somewhere to sit and recover ... Later I would also panic in lectures ... I had a few attacks when outside; usually in hot, stuffy and disorientatingly large shops or when I had to stand around waiting for someone.' JANE S-T.

Situation

Some people panic because of the situation they are put in. Some panic if they find themselves trapped in a room where they can't see the exit. For them safety means knowing where an 'escape route' is, in case the panic starts. Others panic if trapped for a period of time such as having a doctor's or dentist's appointment. For these people safety means avoiding these situations, or trying not to commit themselves to things. Some panic if they have to carry out stressful things alone. For them safety means only doing things with a husband, trusted friend or relative. Here are a few illustrations.

TRAPPED IN A ROOM

'As a newspaper reporter I found the problems of attending crowded council meetings in stuffy committee rooms with no easy avenue of escape to be quite overwhelming, particularly when I had to leave the room for a fourth or fifth time to attend to the needs of acute panic (going to the toilet).' RUTH HURST VOSE, FROM HER BOOK AGORAPHOBIA[10]

TRAPPED FOR A FIXED TIME

'When I was in an exam on 12th March my hands went shaky, I broke out in a cold sweat, and felt physically sick. I felt I'd go out of control and worried I'd start screaming. I had a panic feeling ... a feeling like running.' RON H.

BEING ALONE

'If there's nobody in the house, or my husband's not speaking to me or anything like that, my body starts panicking and I feel like saying to myself, "well I'll disappear" ... I feel like disappearing ... getting away you know. I just feel like running away.' PENNY G.

Feelings

What sets a panic attack off for many sufferers is experiencing feelings in their body. This may include feeling hot, sweating, heart beating faster and dizzy feelings. Often these feelings are set off by quite normal events, though sufferers do not realize this at the time. They may sweat because the room is hotter, or their hearts may beat faster because they are walking, or they may feel dizzy because they are hungry. Other sensations that may worry them are going from dark to light places, higher atmospheric pressure, neon lighting, the surface and texture of floors or feelings of fullness after a meal.

22

Having the flu very often sets off panic because the feelings—lightheadedness, sweatiness and fever—resemble a panic attack very closely; usually sufferers don't recognize that it's simply the flu. For some, *any* change in bodily sensations is enough to set off panic. One man I saw for therapy had given up cigarettes, never took alcohol and refused to take any medication for his very severe panic. He said:

'I'm scared of drugs. I hate having an induced feeling put on me. I panic as soon as I get a feeling that's not happening naturally. If it comes from alcohol I would panic even if the feelings are positive ones. I stopped the cigarettes for one reason (health), but for another really—fear.' JOHN S.

For these people safety means trying to avoid having the feelings they fear. This may mean always keeping cool, trying to avoid sweating by keeping the windows open (very annoying for the rest of the family), trying to stop raised heart rate by walking slowly upstairs, and avoiding 'bloated feelings' by never eating large meals. It generally means that they have to be very careful not to set off certain feelings. They may also take medication to reduce feelings, such as beta-blockers which slow down heart rate. If they are unsuccessful in their attempts to avoid having feelings they also have up their sleeves things they can do to neutralize the unwanted feelings. These include lying very still, going out into the cool fresh air, relaxation and taking bicarbonate.

Anticipation

Some panic sufferers experience panic before they have to do something difficult, in the build-up period. Many find a planned holiday excruciating as the time for departure approaches. The anxiety in waiting is usually worse than the event itself but by the time they get to the event they have exhausted themselves so much they have little strength to deal with the panic. For these people, avoidance means never committing themselves to doing things but going on the spur of the moment. If they feel an attack coming on they may cancel even quite expensive events, such as holidays, and become embarrassed about having to lie or make excuses to others for opting out.

'The unpleasant symptoms of fear which I thought to be symptoms of illness would strike whenever I ventured out, because I had been conditioned like the famous Pavlov's dogs, to expecting them to occur. In fact, sometimes the symptoms would be provoked simply by the knowledge that I had to leave the house.'
PAULINE MCKINNON, FROM IN STILLNESS CONQUER FEAR[11]

'We were going out for an Indian meal. It was a hen night. I was getting ready to go out when it started. The thought of rushing about.'
PAULINE L.

Actions/Lack of Actions

The fifth main pattern of panic is to do with things the person does, or doesn't do. Panic attacks may occur as the person watches television, relaxes, hears an argument, runs up the stairs or has sexual intercourse. For these people, 'safety' is doing something to help, such as lying down, running on the spot, sitting down, tensing up, deep breathing. It may also mean not doing certain things such as purposely not relaxing, not watching certain things on TV, not reading certain things in the newspapers, not talking about or listening to some topics such as mental illness or heart attacks.

WATCHING TV
'I was sitting watching TV. I could feel it coming on. I had to get up and iron some clothes. It was getting worse—pain shooting through me ... this can happen when people talk about heart attacks.

My husband has to warn my friends not to talk about it. I'm frightened to pick up the paper ... Sometimes I'm all at peace watching a film on TV when it comes on you.'
ZENA N.

24

'If I've had a lot to drink the night before I have a lot of little panics the next day. Once when it was my last night on the [oil] rigs I was sitting watching a film on the rig when it suddenly came on.'
JAMES R.

HASSLES OR UPSETS

Robert Freedmen, Director of the Behavioral Medicine Laboratory at Detroit[12] reported a study in which panic sufferers reported their panic and anxiety whilst being 'wired' for 24-hour monitoring of heart rate etc. He reports:

Patient J.M. had spent the day at home resting, watching TV and doing minor chores. She reported anxiety ratings of 20 [out of 100] throughout the day. Shortly after 8 p.m. her daughter came home from school and told her that another girl in school had threatened to kill her. J.M. became very upset about this and, at 8.15 p.m., indicated she was having a panic attack [scoring 80 out of 100].

ARGUMENTS

W.T. had just had a telephone conversation with his homosexual lover whom he had been arguing with. This occurred just after he had begun the Medilog recording. At 10.25 a.m. he pressed the event marker to indicate a panic attack. He reported an anxiety rating of 60 [out of 100] and stated that the attack was caused by thinking about his conversation with his lover.

Thoughts about panic

For some people just thinking about panic, hearing about it or reading about it is enough to give them a panic attack. It is rather difficult to avoid thinking certain thoughts but people do try to avoid this by trying to distract their minds, filling their minds with activity, and never allowing themselves to relax or to do nothing.

Here is an example taken from a therapist's session of a woman who panicked just because the subject of panic feelings is being discussed and it makes her think about it.

Therapist:	Now you've got to accept your ability to feel anything.
Patient:	Right.
Therapist:	But the feelings are not...
Patient:	Dr Zane, I think I'm going to have to go out for a minute or two.
Therapist:	Now wait a minute, dear, you can go out if you want to but please explain to me what's happening.
Patient:	Suddenly that wave of fear coming over me... it just makes me relive the panic attack and I fear it's coming on again. My mind slipped away from what you were saying and I was kind of focusing again on the two panic attacks I've had recently and that kind of feeling came over me.

From M.D. Zane[13]

Sleep

The seventh type of panic is connected with sleep. Some people are aware of fast heartbeats, sudden feelings of falling or jolting or frightening feelings of unconsciousness as they drop off. Others awake bathed in sweat, or with a jolt, heart pounding. Some wake up struggling to breathe. Others wake up feeling they are paralyzed (it seems that they are like this for ages, though it doesn't last long).

Persons with this type of panic may try to avoid certain things related to sleep, such as trying to avoid the sensation of dropping off to sleep. Safety means trying to avoid falling asleep, waiting until it is light, or sleeping half sitting up. Many do allow themselves to go to sleep but to reduce 'danger' always ensure that they have someone to sleep next to them, or have pills or a phone at hand 'just in case'. Sleeping tablets, alcohol or milky drinks may also be used just before bed to try to reduce unpleasant feelings.

'Panics initially occurred only at night, as I was falling asleep. It felt as if the bed was shaking rapidly and for some few weeks I wondered whether something could in fact be causing this—a neighbour's washing machine or a heavy lorry on the road outside. Having decided that this was unlikely and realizing that I was actually shaking I began to wonder whether there was some identifiable cause—was I drinking too much coffee, or spending too long crouched over my computer? These explanations did not stand up to closer examination and I then began to consider whether there was something physically wrong with me.

'Around this time, certainly not much earlier, I began to anticipate that the panics would occur. They also became much more severe—they would still start with the feeling that the bed was shaking, but I would also become aware of my heart beat and breathing. Following this warning, there would be a feeling as if something had dropped inside my chest—like a change of gear—and my heart would start pounding, I would feel as if I couldn't get a proper breath, feel dizzy, and break out in sweat. On some occasions I was woken up by this, and was convinced that this was because my breathing had been erratic, and that if I hadn't woken up I would have died.

'There were several nights when I was still awake and panicking at 4 or 5 in the morning, having had two or three attacks, each coming as I was just dropping off to sleep. The attacks varied in how long they lasted, from ten minutes to about half an hour—but it often took me a good hour after this to pluck up the courage to try to sleep again. I am certain that if sleep was not necessary, I would have avoided it altogether.'
JANE S-T.

'It's a scary feeling because … well … I think it was last week I was … I was in my bed and I woke up with a start and couldn't feel my … I felt I was choking … I couldn't feel my body … you know … I seemed to have stiffened up.'   WILMA W.

Although I have talked about seven main types of panic there is overlap between them, and most sufferers experience more than one kind.

Phobias

Phobias, or irrational fears, are very common. There are many different types of phobia including fear of insects, animals, heights, water, vomiting, blood, injections, hospitals, dentists, or meeting and having to talk to other people. For people with phobias, encountering the thing they fear brings on panic pretty much like clockwork. The problem is quite specific and quite predictable—sufferers are reasonably calm at other times but panic once they are near the thing they fear.

The sort of problem mainly discussed in this book involves panic attacks that occur more unpredictably—there seems to be no one obvious object that sets them off. Some psychologists have described panic as a 'portable phobia'. It is not 'out there' like spiders, dogs or bridges; the feared objects are feelings and sensations inside the person.

A survey carried out by Agras, Sylvester and Oliveau in 1969[14] showed that 40 per cent of normal people have a mild phobia, and 8 per cent a moderately severe one that interferes with their lives. Severely phobic persons are usually afraid of the object of fear itself—for example, spiders—and also frightened by the panic and how it might harm them. This book will still have something to offer to people with such phobias, though it was written mainly for those struggling with unexplained panic and anxiety. And some unhappy people suffer with unexpected panic attacks *and* have severe specific phobias too. Life's not fair, is it?

How Panic Changes People

Have you ever seen TV pictures of a coastal town after it has been struck by a hurricane? The force of the wind and waves hits it full on, smashing trees and houses, ruining roads and scattering debris all over the place. After the wind and sea has calmed down there are months of destruction and havoc to deal with in the town. The hurricane may last one day, but the effects last months.

Devastation

Panic is rather like that. Even after the original panics have struck, the sufferer reacts and reacts for a long time after. Let's look at the typical reactions that follow panic attacks.

STEP 1: FEAR STEPS IN

Firstly, the sufferer becomes very afraid of having another attack, and very afraid of what *might* happen during the next attack. A sense of fear, dread, of impending doom creeps over them. For some it may take two or three attacks before they are really scared; for others just one attack. Whereas their life before was normal enough, with its ups and downs, now fear spoils everything and takes away the joy from even those little things that formerly gave them pleasure.

STEP 2: THE INNER FOCUS

Secondly, the sufferer develops an inner focus, shifting their attention away from what is going on around them and beginning to look inwardly. They don't properly concentrate on what others are saying, or the things they are doing, but are too aware of their own feelings. It's as if their gaze was taken off the outside world and focuses on what is happening inside them.

Sufferers begin to notice feelings, sensations, pains—any changes in what is going on in the body. They become 'body conscious'. They begin to notice whether their heart is beating faster—they may check their pulse. They notice if they are sweating more, breathing faster, feeling sick. They check to see if everything is working OK in the body—like a car in for its annual service—every few hours. They are very aware of any sensations that feel like panic. They are so scared of panic happening again that they notice even slight feelings that may have occurred in panic.

The trouble with looking inwards is that our bodies are changing all the time. For instance when we exert effort—walk or run—our heart will beat faster when we stop, quite naturally. But someone who is constantly checking and worrying about bodily changes may especially notice this. People can become 'sensitized' or over aware of just one or a whole range of feelings.

The net result of this inner focus is that people:

▶ unconsciously look out for the feelings they most dislike

▶ are very sensitive to even small amounts of the feeling

▶ are instantly aware of the feelings

▶ keep concentrating on the feelings once they happen.

STEP 3: FEAR OF FEELINGS
Sufferers become afraid of certain feelings. If they think a panic attack was actually a heart attack the feelings they are most afraid of may be increased heart rate, chest pain, sweating or palpitations. If sufferers notice one of these feelings, they may start to be afraid.

One man I saw when I first began treating panic problems was very afraid of chest pains. He believed the 'heart attack' would happen soon after he felt these pains. I asked him to keep an hourly diary of these chest pains over the following week. He came back the next week looking much happier. He had kept a diary and made little graphs of the strength of chest pains at different times during the day. He noticed these pains occurred twenty minutes after drinking coffee or eating a big meal and realized they were indigestion, not an impending heart attack!

People can also become afraid of certain thoughts as well as feelings. For instance they may think, 'I'm going mad,' and become really scared of that thought running through their minds.

STEP 4: THE VICIOUS CIRCLE

Fourthly—and this is one of the keys to why panic attacks can continue to occur repeatedly—sufferers get into a vicious circle (see Figure 2). They may notice changes in their bodies, such as an increased heart rate. If they are afraid that a panic might start, the fear of this can create more feelings—the heart may start beating faster still—which makes them more afraid—which causes the heart to beat even faster. Their fear of panic may actually create a new panic attack. This has been noticed by

Fig. 2: The vicious circle of panic

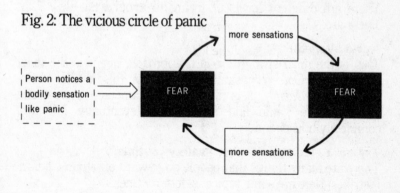

many writers on anxiety. It has been called 'fear of fear', 'fear of bodily sensations', 'negative spiral' and 'negative feedback loop'. Even a thought such as 'I might have a panic' may be enough in one person to start this fear cycle going.

STEP 5: AVOIDANCE
Fifthly, sufferers' fears begin to change their lifestyle. They may start to avoid places or situations in which they have had a panic attack before, or where they reckon they might panic. Alternatively they may try to avoid doing or thinking things that might bring on panic. Figure 3 illustrates this.

Fig. 3: Avoidance patterns

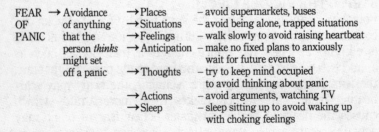

FEAR	→ Avoidance	→ Places	– avoid supermarkets, buses
OF	of anything	→ Situations	– avoid being alone, trapped situations
PANIC	that the	→ Feelings	– walk slowly to avoid raising heartbeat
	person *thinks*	→ Anticipation	– make no fixed plans to anxiously
	might set		wait for future events
	off a panic	→ Thoughts	– try to keep mind occupied
			to avoid thinking about panic
		→ Actions	– avoid arguments, watching TV
		→ Sleep	– sleep sitting up to avoid waking up
			with choking feelings

There are different levels of trying to avoid what they fear. These are:

Avoid altogether
This is the most straightforward approach, but it is the most devastating. One very sad description of this is *The Autobiography of David*[15]. It is the story of a famous journalist and writer whose panic and agoraphobia eventually left him completely housebound.

Try not to let a panic start ('safety routines')
There are many things that people do to ward off a panic before it strikes. Here are some typical safety routines:

- ▶ take pills or alcohol before doing something difficult
- ▶ take a trusted friend
- ▶ hold the hand of a child
- ▶ take a dog or walking stick with them
- ▶ chew peppermints
- ▶ hold themselves tense all the time
- ▶ wear sunglasses
- ▶ keep their mind occupied with other things at all times
- ▶ stay close to walls, or near to doors
- ▶ only tackle things on 'good days'
- ▶ try to psych themselves up with 'you'll be all right, you'll be all right'.

Some therapists call these 'talismans': as long as the person wears a 'magical' token, or does a 'magical' act, they believe they will be safe from harm. People develop hundreds of habits to prevent or avoid panic. One sufferer put it like this:

'Going shopping bears all the resemblance to planning a train robbery. Lines of escape must be worked out all the way, and as long as 'rabbit runs' exist on any outing it can usually be tolerated'
RUTH HURST VOSE, FROM HER BOOK AGORAPHOBIA[10]

Be prepared for the worst ('life-savers')
This is the equivalent of always carrying around a first-aid kit in case disaster strikes. People can develop all sorts of tricks to bring feelings down to a manageable level once they start. Sometimes they take an object—a quarter-bottle of gin in the handbag, smelling salts, a self-help panic leaflet, a portable phone.

Many sufferers keep a few tranquillizers in their purse or pocket 'just in case' panic starts. These are often as much a psychological comfort as a real benefit. One man whom I saw as a patient felt fine when he had to attend a business convention— no anxiety, no panic—until he remembered he had forgotten his 'safety' tranquillizer. Then his panic started. Many sufferers have developed their own list of things they can do which they think will reduce panic once it starts. The list of things is endless: among other things they may lie down on the bed, take a deep breath, drink water, drink alcohol, take valium or some other tranquillizer, try to talk themselves out of it, open a window, go in or out of the house, run, or try to pretend they are not feeling sensations.

Avoidance: live now, pay later

Although it may seem the natural thing to try to avoid, prevent or reduce panic it is only a short-term solution. It brings some relief *now*; but in the long run it only keeps the problem going. The person may think they are pouring water on the fire to put it out, but they've got hold of the wrong can and are pouring petrol on it instead. It is damaging to try to avoid having panic attacks because:

▶ it clutters up the sufferer's life to an incredible degree, narrowing their prospects and generally reducing the quality of their life

▶ it means that if a panic does occur they are unprepared for it and haven't learnt how to cope

▶ it keeps the sufferer from discovering the real truth: what would happen if they made no attempt to avoid, stop or minimize panic.

What *would* happen if the person did not try to fight panic at all? This may be a scary idea but, as following chapters show, it is one of the keys to successful therapy.

4

What Is a Panic Attack?

The human body is an amazing thing. Our bodies seem to be specially designed to save us and help us deal with harm. Take a cut on the finger—why doesn't the blood keep pouring out until we are dead? The body recognizes there is a cut and things change. When the blood comes into contact with the air it reacts differently and starts to clot up. The blood gets thicker and thicker and eventually forms a scab. After a few days even that drops off and the whole thing is healed up. It works like clockwork; it doesn't matter if we are asleep or awake, unintelligent or a genius—the body heals up just the same. Automatically.

What happens if food or drink accidentally 'goes down the wrong way'—into the windpipe? We automatically cough and splutter. What does this do? It shoots the food or drink out of the windpipe at a great speed. We keep on coughing until the unwanted food is safely out of our windpipe. We don't have to stop and think 'food in the windpipe is dangerous to the lungs—I must expel it'; the body automatically takes over and does the right thing—cough.

What if we eat some food that's going bad, or poisonous? The stomach automatically detects that something is wrong and shoots the food back up again—we're sick, we vomit—it's not pleasant but it does the trick—the food is out of our system.

When we catch an illness such as the flu, germs are detected in the body and special cells named antibodies are produced to surround the germs and 'smother' them. Each time we get a new illness, new antibodies are created which can deal with that particular germ next time. The way in which antibodies work is so complicated it has taken researchers years to discover and there is still more to find out. Yet the smallest child can produce antibodies without thinking. Our bodies are working day and night for our protection. The amazing thing is that it is all automatic.

I've just used these four examples of how the body automatically looks after us. But there are thousands of ways it is trying to protect us. A hundred modern computers could not look after us as cleverly as our bodies can. In this chapter I will be describing panic and anxiety symptoms but as I do, I want us to keep firmly in mind that the body is an amazing protective machine, working for us even when things go wrong.

The fear reaction

One automatic type of protection in the body is the fear reaction. Let's say we are walking down a narrow alley way when suddenly two snarling Rottweilers leap out at us, barking, with teeth flashing and saliva running down their jaws. Do we reason out: 'This is a dog. It is snarling. It is biting my hand. I am in danger. I should take effective action. What should I do? Yes, I think running is the best solution.' No, not at all! We'd probably be mauled to death before we finished the thought process. No, what happens is that our body automatically reacts ultra-quickly. Adrenalin is pumped into the bloodstream; our heart pounds, we break out in a sweat and before we have time to think—in an instant—we are either fleeing like the wind or fighting the dogs off like a demon. This is the fear reaction. It is there to save us from harm.

We run like the wind away from the dogs. They are right behind us snapping and snarling but we really move pretty quickly and get away. When we've run about a hundred yards and reckon it's safe enough to stop, we turn round to see if they've stopped chasing us. What do we notice about our bodies?

▶ Our hearts are beating like a train engine. Fast and hard.

▶ Our breathing is fast and deep.

▶ We are trembling and shaking and sweating all over.

▶ Our mouths are dry as a bone.

▶ We feel a bit sick and dizzy.

▶ Our hands and feet are tingling.

▶ We are really very aroused, tense and alert, watching out for new danger.

Are we afraid? Well we *were* afraid of the dogs but now they seem to have settled down and are barking in the distance. We are not the least bit afraid of these changes in our bodies—even though there are many changes and the feelings are very strong. The feelings themselves do not bother us because we know exactly why we are feeling them. They are part of our reaction to fear. In a few minutes, when the adrenalin has broken down in our blood stream, the body sensations will gradually disappear. We will not be thinking too much about our feelings because we know the reason for them. The fear reaction is there to protect us from danger; actually if we'd recorded our hundred metres' dash we'd have discovered it was a personal best. The fear reaction gives us that extra strength needed to escape from danger.

The fear reaction is at the heart of a panic attack. The sensations involved in the fear reaction and panic are exactly the same—fast heartbeat, increased breathing, sweating, trembling, dry mouth, tingling hands and feet and so on. Not all these sensations may occur in one panic attack and different people notice different feelings. But basically the reaction is the same. The only difference—and this is a big difference—is that we know why we reacted the way we did to the dogs.

Although a panic attack is exactly the same as the fear reaction, there is no obvious trigger or stimulus, such as a snarling dog or an attacker to set off the strong feelings. No wonder people with panic are completely bewildered. They cannot see a reason for their powerful feelings and start to think of heart attacks, brain tumours, mental breakdown, losing control and so on. The fear reaction is such a strong one that a sufferer feels there must be some reason and it must be really serious. I think most people faced with strong feelings out of the blue would be really worried that something serious was going on. It is quite natural to think like this.

What has actually happened in panic attack is that the body's normal fear reaction has been switched on by accident.

The fear reaction blow by blow

Coming back to my original point: the body is designed to protect us. Every part of the fear reaction is there for a reason—to help us survive. None of the feelings is at all harmful—quite the opposite; they are there for our protection. It is the same with panic—none of the feelings can harm us. I will now go through the different symptoms of panic anxiety showing what the reason is for each feeling.

Figure 4 shows the different parts of the body that are involved in the fear reaction.

Fig. 4: The fear reaction

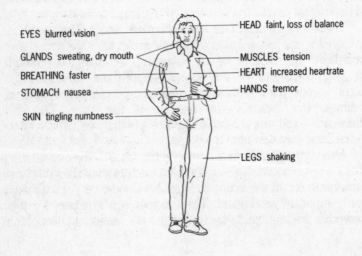

EYES blurred vision

GLANDS sweating, dry mouth

BREATHING faster

STOMACH nausea

SKIN tingling numbness

HEAD faint, loss of balance

MUSCLES tension

HEART increased heartrate

HANDS tremor

LEGS shaking

HEART

'Surges of fear rippled through my body. I knew this time I would not come out of it, I'll definitely die this time. Gasping for breath, my heart seemed to thump. I would feel it to see if it had stopped. It seemed to jump inside of me.'   S.R.

Panic and anxiety usually involve an increased rate of heartbeats. 85 per cent of panic sufferers report pounding of the heart in panic. For some people awareness of the heartbeat becomes the main problem. The heart beats faster and can give the impression of beating harder. Sometimes it is irregular or a beat is missed. A sufferer might feel the veins throbbing in their neck. Pain or pressure in the chest may be felt. Sometimes people are aware of fast heartbeats as they are dropping off to sleep. Others suddenly awake in the night with palpitations.

Why should increased heart rate be useful to us? The heart is crucial because it pumps blood with its vital supplies of oxygen to every part of the body, right to the outermost parts of the skin. Every part of the body needs oxygen. If we are to fight like a tiger or run like the wind, the extra oxygen in the blood must be sent quickly to the most important parts of the body, such as the arm and leg muscles. To do this the heart must beat much faster.

STOMACH

'I get a funny feeling in my stomach and I seem to want to run away...ah...it's a queer feeling, you know.'   EDWARD P.

In danger, who needs to digest their food? The body diverts blood away from the less important parts, the stomach and gut, to feed the more important parts, the muscles of the arms and thighs, so that we can run fast. This can give a nauseous feeling—butterflies in the stomach—or a rumbling stomach. Bowels and bladder get ready to empty, giving feelings of wanting to rush to the toilet (although people don't actually empty their bladder in panic).

SKIN

Blood is reduced from the skin, fingers and toes so that it can flow into the arms and legs. We may seem to go paler, feel as if the blood is draining away from us or get tingling sensations or numb feelings in the outer parts of our body. Apart from increasing blood flow to the muscles, cutting down blood to the skin is also very useful if we are seriously cut or gashed. Less blood is lost.

BREATHING

'Already I was finding it difficult to breathe and the horrible feelings in my stomach started. It was horrible not being able to breathe, I was gasping for air, then I would start noticing the street and houses looking strange.'   T.I.

In panic our breathing speeds up and gets deeper. It needs to do this to get oxygen into the lungs (which are surrounded by blood vessels), to get it into the blood so that, once in the bloodstream, it can be taken to the muscles. This results in feeling short of breath or smothering sensations. 53 per cent of panic sufferers report breathing difficulties in panic and 48 per cent smothering sensations. The chest wall tightens, causing feelings of pressure or pain in the chest or a heavy feeling. Some people think that they can't get enough air into their lungs and try desperately hard to suck in more air. If the oxygen we breath in is not used up by fighting or running, then we will have too much oxygen in our blood, causing some unusual sensations such as tingling in the fingers or toes (38 per cent), light-headedness or unreality feelings (45 per cent). Fear of not getting enough air in and taking deeper breaths to make up for it actually gives us too much oxygen.

In what way is this useful to us in fear? If we are to run fast we must get as much oxygen to our body as possible. Fast and deep breathing does that. You sometimes see athletes deep-breathing before a race to increase oxygen to their bodies, to help their performance.

SHAKING

'I went into the bingo and I couldna concentrate. My hands started shaking. I tried to mark the number off the card. I couldna do it and I telt mysel, "dinna be so stupid". I couldna see the number you know and my hands started shakin and everything.' ANN P.

Trembling and shaking occurs in 70 per cent of panic sufferers. It is simply a result of adrenalin, increased arousal and having the energy and tension to cope with danger but no outlet for it.

If we do not run or fight then too much oxygen goes to our legs and arms, making them tremble or shake or giving us wobbly or rubber legs. This is uncomfortable and baffling if we are just sitting still, as we are not using up the energy that nature has provided us with.

Some people with panic have learned a little trick of running fast when they panic—they say it makes them feel better, though it might make other people a bit bewildered! It uses up the extra energy and makes them feel better, but I don't recommend it as a cure for panic. It just locks people into a 'we-gotta-get-out-of-here' routine whenever the first few flickering signs of panic come on.

SWEATING

Our glands are part of our fear reaction. We sweat or go hot and cold to stop us overheating and to keep the body's temperature the same—just like a thermostat. 62 per cent of panic sufferers report sweating in panic and 56 per cent having hot flushes (if you live in the United States you don't have hot flushes—it's hot flashes!). The saliva glands in the mouth dry up, making the mouth feel dry. Occasionally people will complain of a strange taste in their mouth like a metallic or minty taste. Particular body odours may be produced.

TENSION, CHOKING SENSATIONS AND PROBLEMS SWALLOWING

People may feel certain muscles in the body tense up, such as tenseness in the arms and legs or feeling a knot in the stomach or tightness across the neck or chest. Tenseness occurs in 68 per cent of panic sufferers. A tenseness in the throat added to rapid breathing, drying of the saliva glands and the coating of the throat sometimes creates choking sensations (61 per cent) or the feeling of not being able to swallow properly.

The increased activity of the muscles can also produce a twitching sensation or trembling. To run or fight, our bodies need to be tense. We don't need to eat when we are escaping for our lives, so we don't need saliva which is basically in our mouths for the purpose of making it easier to swallow our food.

HEAD AND EYES

Often in panic (48 per cent of sufferers) people feel giddy or dizzy, with loss of balance or unsteadiness, feeling that they might fall over. They quite often hold onto something to steady themselves. One man I was treating clung to a bollard to stop himself (as he thought) falling over.

Sometimes in panic people experience blurred or distorted vision; some complain that it is impossible to read close up.

Have you ever been to an eye specialist who puts a few drops of liquid into your eye so that your pupil stays wide open and he can examine your eye more easily? Afterwards your pupils are still wide open and the world seems a bit strange; you are very sensitive to light; it hurts your eyes; you can't read and you feel unsteady when you walk. You want to hide in a dark corner until your pupils start to work properly again.

In the fear reaction the pupils open wide—the reaction comes from adrenalin inside the body rather than from anyone putting drops into the eyes. This causes more light to flood into our eyes, which is useful to help take in as much of the surroundings as possible in order to spot danger. The muscles at the side of the eyes which make the eyes focus (ciliary muscles) also tense up, making us focus best on things between three and ten metres away. This is very helpful in battle or if you are attacked by animals but not very useful if you are an office worker trying to read close up. The body seems to have reckoned that, where danger is concerned, it's most important to focus on the middle distance.

OVER-SENSITIVITY

'I became acutely hyper-sensitive, unable to stand noise, movement, touch, watching television, the feel of the sheets on my bed, or even the feel of the hair on my head.' J.S.

In anxiety people can feel much more alert and sensitive to sounds and light than usual. The telephone rings and they are startled and jump up very easily. Feeling so alert can also make people irritable with their families. The story is told of two soldiers back in England from a spell of duty in Northern Ireland who were walking down the street; a car backfired and both immediately hit the pavement. It's very useful to be hyper-sensitive when bullets are flying and danger is around every corner. Adrenalin makes our bodies race faster and our hearing and vision more sensitive. It helps in running and spotting danger but, if we don't use it up, everything can seem to pound away too fast and make the world overwhelming.

DREAD

Sometimes people in panic feel a terrible sense of dread or impending doom. As the fear reaction is all about spotting and getting away from death and injury it is not surprising that feelings of doom or destruction come with the package. On top of this is the sufferers' dread of what might happen to them in panic.

LOSS OF CONCENTRATION

'I'm trying to listen to the conversation that's going on because you sort of start to drift as you're so intent on yourself. You're drifting into a little world of your own—how you feel and your palpitations and everything.' Y.A.

Being able to concentrate on things such as reading or conversations becomes very difficult, because so much energy is taken up concentrating on bodily feelings.

When panicking, people may also feel that they are not able to control their thoughts and judgments and generally that their thoughts are racing too fast. This is not surprising, as the fear reaction makes us really alert and speeds up the body in many ways, including our thinking. We need to concentrate on where the danger is, and how to escape from it, with all our attention and not bother about logical thought or making well-informed judgments. Again, it seems to be a case of our mind being 'pre-set' into danger mode—blow all the fancy intellectual stuff!

UNREALITY FEELINGS

Feelings of unreality or 'de-personalization' occur in about 15 to 20 per cent of panic sufferers. They feel that the world is unreal or strange or that they have changed as a person. One man said 'I felt slightly unreal and as though I wasn't part of my surroundings but watching from a distance; my voice sounded strange to me and did not seem part of me.' These are very frightening sensations and can sap a person's sense of confidence. Some experts think that unreality feelings are a way of emotionally cutting oneself off from danger, though this isn't certain.

Is the fear reaction safe?

There are other feelings which are part of the fear reaction that I have not mentioned in this chapter, but I have tried to cover the main feelings. They really occur and are not imaginary, but they all exist for one purpose, basically to protect us from danger. In panic many sufferers think that because the feelings are very strong they must also be very dangerous. But what would be the point of having an automatic fear reaction that could do us harm? The fantastic protective system which could help us to react quickly enough to save us from being mauled by a lion could then kill us when we had safely got away! It would make no sense at all. Yes, these feelings are strong—they need to be, to shift us out of danger. But in themselves they are not at all dangerous.

Secondary reactions to having panic attacks

Some feelings are not part of the fear reaction, but occur as a secondary result of it. For instance, despair can be caused by the misery of panic attacks. If someone's life is suddenly ruined by these panic attacks it is normal enough for them to feel that the future is hopeless. Here are three important secondary reactions.

INTRUSIVE THOUGHTS

Intrusive thoughts can be very distressing indeed. These thoughts keep coming into the sufferer's mind against their will. They are exactly the opposite to what the person wants to think. They seem to attack the things the person loves most or holds most sacred. For instance, a mother who loves her baby may get thoughts that she might stab or strangle the baby, which of course are most horrible to her. A husband may get thoughts that he might harm his wife. There may be thoughts that the sufferer will do something foolish to ruin their career. These thoughts have an impulsive feeling about them, and people get very afraid if they really believe they will carry out such plans, but they are just thoughts. They are an exaggeration of normal reactions.

People who are afraid of these thoughts often try to push them from their minds. The effort involved in doing this really means that they are spending a lot of time concentrating on the thoughts, making them more likely to intrude. Pleasant intrusive thoughts occur with many people (for instance, about sex) but they don't usually worry about having them and don't try to push them away. It is not surprising that during a period of strain and panic more unpleasant thoughts are likely, and this can be frightening.

FORGETFULNESS

One quite common part of anxiety is forgetfulness. It is not permanent, although the person concerned often thinks it is a sign that they are losing their mind. Partly, forgetfulness occurs because they are preoccupied with their feelings and problems and other ordinary concerns pale into insignificance. Also, a person who sees forgetfulness as a sign that they are 'losing their marbles' may worry more than is necessary. They may notice occasions when they have forgotten things, whereas previously they wouldn't even have thought about it.

EXHAUSTION

'Putting up with the constant dragging terror saps energy on a massive scale. This results in everyday jobs assuming gigantic proportions, where even to put a load of washing in a machine seems an almost insuperable task.' C.F.

The sufferer becomes tired of fighting and resisting panic feelings, and has little energy left for daily living.

Please take away my fear

In this chapter I have tried to cover most of the sensations felt by people with panic attacks. They won't all occur in one person but I needed to make the list as long as possible to try to cover most of the feelings that bother people. Panic sufferers at times wish that all these feelings would go away, never to return, or that they could somehow be removed from them, as a surgeon would remove a cancer. However if we could remove our fear reaction altogether we would probably be taking away our own life. The problem is that it is being triggered off at the wrong time. I must stress that, in themselves, the body's reactions are natural and completely harmless, though very frightening when the person concerned cannot see what is causing them. An added source of fear is the myths that surround panic, some of which I shall examine in Part II.

PART II

Myths About Panic

5

What a Panic Isn't!

At its heart, fear is based on the belief that danger is about to occur. One person panicking is afraid of a heart attack occurring, but another is afraid of losing control of the mind and having a nervous breakdown. The idea of danger is always lurking, but different people imagine different types of danger during a panic.

A case of mistaken identity

Sometimes we make mistakes. Take the man on the underground station in London during the rush hour. A train arrived. It was absolutely jam-packed with people. But he thought he might just be able to squeeze in—so he did. As he stood with his back to the doors waiting for them to close, much to his amazement someone else pushed in and stood behind him. As he stood there he felt a cold steel point against his back. He had heard about muggings and violence on the Underground. Was he about to be murdered? Was he being asked to hand over his wallet? A cold sweat broke out on his brow. He started to shake. He slowly struggled to turn and face the fierce mugger, fearing that any moment the knife might pierce through his back ... and then ... he saw something that quite surprised him. It was a little old lady cramped behind him with the point of her umbrella poking in his back. He had made a mistake.

All the time that man believed there was an mugger with a knife behind him, he sweated, he trembled, his heart raced—he was afraid. On seeing the little old lady his emotions immediately changed; he was filled with relief, and felt foolish about how he could have made such a silly mistake.

Let me suggest something to you that you may find quite difficult to accept: that a panic attack is basically like that little old lady. Terrifying and terrible, when the person doesn't know what it is, but absolutely harmless when you know the real cause.

But panic seems such a terrible experience. Something awful must be happening.

Yes, the experience of panic is terrifying. Yes, the feelings are very strong. Yes, it seems to occur for no reason. Yes, sufferers feel they must do something to stop it happening. But it is a case of mistaken identity. The attack cannot lead to a nervous breakdown, a stroke, a heart attack. People do not lose control, pass out, or make fools of themselves. It feels as if these things are true, but they are simply not. In the next two chapters I want to explore in some detail the myths that people come to believe about panic.

Myth No. 1: 'It's never going to end'

Let's take one of the commonest fears first, that the experience of panic will never end. Panic feelings arise suddenly, and keep getting stronger and stronger until sufferers feel they must do something to escape or stop the feelings. They might run out of shops, if that is where panic is worse, sit down or lie down, do something distracting, call the doctor or take tranquillizers—anything to stop panic mounting. When they start to calm down they are left with the impression that the attack would have gone on and on, increasing to breaking point, if they had not done whatever it was they did that seemed to stop it. This though, is an impression. What is the truth?

What is a normal panic attack? Figure 5 (over the page) shows what happens during panic. Panic feelings rise up to an almost unbearable level where the sufferer can't seem to think straight and just wants to escape (the body's fear reaction).

49

However if the sufferer does not escape but just faces their fear, panic feelings gradually subside of their own accord.

Fig. 5: A normal panic attack

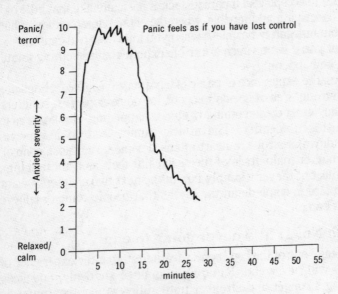

Some facts and figures

Based on three psychological studies[16, 17, 18] in which panic sufferers recorded what was happening to them before and after panic attacks, the average length of attack was twenty-four minutes. 17 per cent of sufferers had attacks of less than five minutes, 40 per cent less than ten minutes, 75 per cent less than thirty minutes and 90 per cent less than one hour.

The body brings panic to a natural end. For the small number of individuals who have panic attacks over thirty minutes, I have often found that their very attempts to fight off panic attacks are the main reason that they go on for so long. They struggle and fight, try to do things to stop the panic, or try to analyze it. These attempts to stop or stifle panic only serve to keep it going longer than it would naturally, and of course this fighting makes the person exhausted. Surrendering to the experience without fighting allows panic to run its natural course. Claire Weekes, who has written some of the best books on anxiety (see Recommended Reading), likens this to allowing oneself to be carried along by a wave in the sea rather than trying to swim against it.

A panic attack is in many ways like crying. Supposing a workmate or friend has died. You might feel like crying that evening when thinking about it in the quietness of your own home. That is quite normal. If you let yourself cry you might continue to cry for several minutes or even longer. But even though the feelings are very strong they will eventually calm down. Once you get it out of your system, you automatically stop crying. Let it take its own course and you run out of steam. But what if you fight your grief and try to hold the tears back? You might be successful for a while but then the desire to cry returns. You fight it again—it stops, only to return later. This way you can keep the feelings going for hours. In other words fight the feelings and they seem to keep coming; but surrender to the feelings, let them run their natural course, and they are over much quicker. It is exactly so with panic. Panic is a time-limited response.

6

Death and Physical Illness Myths

The next three chapters try to cover all the main fears about panic attacks. This means that they are crammed full with information. Please feel free just to read the bits that apply most to you.

Myth No. 2: 'It's my heart'

'I will have a heart attack. This is the big one. This is the one that will kill me.'

Panic attacks in many ways give the impression of a heart attack. Palpitations, chest pain, sweating and breathlessness are common. Panic attacks used to be called 'cardiac neuroses' because of their close link with heart symptoms. After a first panic attack, sufferers often contact their local doctor who comes round on an emergency visit to check the (conscious) person over. Much to the sufferer's bewilderment their doctor cannot find a great deal wrong with them. They do not fit the usual pattern of symptoms for a heart attack. However, 'nothing is wrong with you' does not satisfy the sufferer who has just experienced such a terrible attack; and under pressure, or to be on the safe side, the doctor may refer the patient to a specialist cardiologist.

After the usual delays the person goes through all the tests and the cardiologist reports back to the doctor that there is no heart problem—maybe a slight arrythmia ('skipped' heartbeats) or slightly raised electro-cardiograph (ECG) reading, but nothing clinically significant. The doctor then tells the sufferer that there was a slightly raised ECG but nothing clinically wrong.

The sufferer may take away the impression that there is something serious or undetected, that the doctors don't know what they are talking about, or that something is being hidden from them, and may still harbour the belief that it is a heart condition. And a sufferer given an absolutely clean bill of health is just left bewildered. It had all the feeling of a heart condition— what was it, then?

'It's all in the mind' is unfortunately a phrase that people use about anxiety. Often the sufferer thinks this means 'it's all imaginary'. They try very hard to accept that they have imagined this attack, even to the point of doubting their own sanity. But the feelings were absolutely real—my heart did race—I was breathless—how can this be imaginary?

Of course, the feelings are not imaginary—temperature change, sweating, increased heart rate can all be measured in the laboratory during panic attacks; these things actually do occur. 'It's all in the mind' should really be translated as 'the *causes* are psychological', or 'the causes are in the mind'. The panic reactions are all very physical and very real, but the causes are emotional, not a physical disease.

How can you tell the difference between a heart attack and a panic attack? After all, chest pain, increased heart rate and breathlessness occur in both conditions. 'Chest pain is one of the most characteristic and valuable symptoms in diagnosing coronary heart disease,' says Dr P. Kezdi, Professor of Medicine at Wright State University School of Medicine, 'but is at the same time the most misunderstood symptom. There are some 101 different causes of chest pain, and coronary heart disease is only one of them.'

'There are early warning signals of heart disease and there are also false signals. As so often in human behaviour, frequently we ignore the true warning signals while being over-concerned about the false signals. Let us therefore stress here that there is no way that you

alone can determine the true meaning of a symptom or signal. To do so you need the interpretation of an expert, your doctor.[19]

In other words, people should not get carried away by their own diagnosis based on chest pain or palpitations, but on what their doctor or the heart specialist tells them about their heart. Specialists do know what they are talking about! There are, however, certain things which may suggest we are experiencing panic attacks rather than heart attacks.

If they occur in specific situations—such as relaxing in the evening, waiting in queues, thinking about our problems, after a domestic argument—or in particular places—such as shops, buses, queues, church, lifts or hairdressers—they are very likely to be panic attacks and not heart attacks. Panic is tied to certain cues (even if the person hasn't identified them all); heart attacks are not so closely tied to situations or events.

The one exception to this is exercise. Symptoms of heart disease can be worse the harder one exercises. Panic attacks can also occur during exercise, but they usually occur at other times too. During exercise, such as walking upstairs or walking rather quickly on a cold morning, one's heart is bound to beat faster and harder and breathing will be faster and deeper. That is only natural, but if this is the only time chest pain[*] occurs, the person concerned should get a doctor's opinion on whether this might be a genuine heart condition. However, if the person has had a racing heart for some time and is still alive and otherwise physically well, it is more likely to be panic.

Above all, the doctor's opinion as to whether or not someone has heart problems is more reliable than their own opinion. One patient I was seeing was terrified of her heart symptoms. She had pain radiating down her right arm and was convinced it was a heart attack. She had to laugh at herself when I informed her that in heart attacks pain radiates down the left arm!

* Chest pain refers to heaviness or pressure behind the breast bone, or aching or burning between the shoulder blades, sometimes radiating to the neck, jaw, left shoulder and inside surface of the arm down to the elbow.

Another lady I treated typically had panic attacks in bed at night—she thought they were heart attacks and would get up and get dressed and drive eighteen miles during the night, parking outside the city Accident and Emergency Department. She did this so that when her heart attack occurred, specialist help would be available. She had been doing this for ten years! I explained to her the importance of putting this wrong idea to the test. This meant she had to stay in bed and let herself 'die' there. It was almost impossible for her to contemplate this horror. But she gradually came round to the suggestion, and after one of our therapy sessions summoned up her courage and decided to go ahead and 'die'.

It may sound funny but to her death was more than likely, so it took great courage for her to agree to my suggestion. After a few excruciating nights of allowing 'heart attacks' to occur without trying to ward them off or escape to the safety of the local hospital she realized that she was still alive and had been fundamentally mistaken about the 'heart attacks'. After that the panic attacks got fewer and weaker.

Myth No. 3: 'I will die'

Over many years my colleagues and I have kept people company when they have had panic attacks. This is distressing for the sufferer, and often for the therapist too. I have never found any serious] physical effects from panic, and people certainly do not die from panic. I have searched the research documents, attended conferences, and talked to colleagues, yet have never come across one instance of death from an individual panic attack—and this surely would have been reported.

Some people are afraid that their panic is so strong, so tremendously powerful, that it is bound to cause physical or mental damage—it might set off a heart attack or a stroke. But the body seems to withstand panic attacks perfectly well, time after time, and for long periods of time. The chemicals released into the blood during panic, including adrenalin, are naturally produced by the body, and are basically there to protect it, not to harm it. As Claire Weekes explains in *Peace from Nervous Suffering*, 'If you could see how thick, and appreciate how powerful your heart muscle is, you would lose all fear of its bursting or being damaged by palpitations'[20]. In the same way, though someone may feel pressure or pain inside or around their head, and can feel the veins of their forehead strongly pulsating, the veins cannot burst or cause a leak inside the brain or a brain tumour.

Although it is impossible to die from a panic attack itself, if the person has a pre-existing physical problem such as a history of heart failure or severe asthma, then a panic attack, like other sorts of exertion, might set off their other condition. If a GP refers people to me for therapy who are suffering from both panic attacks and a diagnosed physical problem I usually ask the GP's opinion as to whether they should be encouraged to go through a panic. Most often the view is that the person will experience a lot more panic if left without therapy; overcoming their fear offers them the best chance overall. In cases like these, which are the exception rather than the rule, a gradual approach to the problem may be more appropriate, in which the person only faces fear a little bit at a time.

Myth No. 4: 'I will pass out'

As feelings get stronger, especially light-headedness, dizziness, nausea, and blurred vision, sufferers are sure that they will fall over or pass out—absolutely sure. They steady themselves, or sit down to stop this happening. Other people believe them too; shop assistants or helpful partners find a chair for them or help to get them into the fresh air. I have even come across some self-help books on anxiety that misinform readers that 'the worst that can happen is that you will pass out'. People do not pass out with panic.

Someone may say, 'I remember five years ago when I did pass out.' But did they really pass out? Or nearly pass out? Were they *actually* unconscious? People may actually have fainted in the past because of some other physical cause—such as passing out in pregnancy, because of high blood pressure or anaemia, after a sauna, or standing up too quickly—not due to the panic attack itself. These physical causes may not be present now, but because sufferers have fainted in the past they may assume they will still pass out. However, it is impossible to pass out from panic attacks.

There is one exception to this rule. It concerns people who are extremely anxious with anything to do with medical matters—hospitals, injections, the sight of blood. Usually in panic attacks the body is getting more worked up and tense as the heart rate speeds up, breathing gets faster, sweating increases and so on, and therefore the blood pressure goes up. However, it is when blood pressure goes down that a person can pass out.

When some individuals see blood, their heart rate and blood pressure go down. It is not only in comedy films that medical students new to the operating theatre pass out at the sight of blood; in real life too, people can pass out at the sight of blood or injections. In time they can learn to overcome this, as some surgeons will tell you. However, this exception to the rule only occurs in a small percentage of people. During panic attacks a tensed-up person cannot possibly reach such a pitch that they pass out; the body doesn't work like that. They are too up-tight, aroused, and over-reacting to be able to faint.

When I wrote the first draft of this chapter, discussing passing out due to panic, I said, 'there are two small exceptions to the rule.' The second exception I was going to describe was for those people who seriously overbreathe during panic. Then I came across an interesting study by three Dutch researchers[21]. They instructed twenty volunteers to forcefully overbreathe for ninety minutes or more. They report: 'All our subjects hyperventilated to a degree that is about the maximum that human subjects can accomplish (a reduction in carbon dioxide by 55 per cent) and they did so for one and a half hours. None of them fainted and none of them died.' This suggests that it is almost impossible to pass out even with serious hyperventilation, even though the person may feel light-headed.

Myth No. 5: 'I am going to have a stroke'

A person may mistake a panic attack for a stroke, or think it will reach such terrible heights that they will have a stroke. Others are more afraid about how they will be left after this supposed stroke: they will become 'vegetables', unable to cope for themselves, talk or feed themselves, with others having to take them to the toilet. Often they have observed some elderly relative after a stroke, or physically deteriorating in a home or hospital, which has made such an impression on them as to set off a secret fear that this may someday happen to them. Having to depend on others is a terrible thought to them; and needless to say their fear causes them to take a massive leap in their imagination so that they see themselves totally incapacitated by a panic attack. But no such thing actually happens.

Myth No. 6: 'Something's wrong with my eyes'

'What really got me going were those terrible moments when my vision suddenly went blurred and my heart would leap almost into my throat. Phew, that's awful.'

Feelings such as blurred vision, not being able to focus properly or a general feeling that things are swimming around can lead people to think they have some serious problem with their eyes or are going blind. I have never treated a person made blind by panic. I have never read of a person made blind through panic. I have never met a blind person whose blindness was caused by panic. It would be extremely difficult to understand how the optic nerve, a very tough and thick fibre, could be harmed in the slightest way by a fear reaction. I have seen plenty of people with a fear of blurred vision and what it signifies, but no permanent harm can be done to the eye by panic attacks.

7

The Destroyed-By-Your-Own-Body Myths

Chapter 4 talked about the perfect design of the body. The destroyed-by-your-own-body myths work almost in reverse. Instead of the body being there to protect, preserve and help us it is seen as an enemy. During a panic attack the sufferer becomes afraid about some vital aspect of the body's functioning such as not being able to breathe, swallow or move. Their attention may focus on this area of the body and create a vicious circle in two ways:

▶ They may try to compensate; for instance if they feel they cannot get enough air in they may try to suck or gulp in more air. This 'compensation' actually increases the discomfort and interferes with the natural (automatic) working of the body.

▶ Fear of not being able to breathe, swallow, urinate and so on actually creates more of the feelings of which they are afraid. For instance fear of not being able to swallow dries up the saliva, making it more difficult to swallow—a self-fulfilling prophecy.

Myth No. 7: 'I'll be paralyzed'

'I was into Woolworths and then I went up the stairs to get this message [item of shopping]. I looked round and there was a crowd of people. I picked up the item and was about to move to the counter to pay for it and I couldn't move. I felt my legs like lead!'   J.ST.

A feeling of paralysis and a fear that it might continue to some very dangerous point occurs with some panic sufferers. Again, these are fears of what might happen but does not occur. They are based on brief sensations of being paralyzed which are misunderstood and blown out of proportion. For instance, it is quite a common experience for ordinary people to wake from sleep with a feeling of paralysis—that they cannot move or breath. It is very unpleasant, but is only a passing feeling which disappears as they wake properly. If someone starts to believe they really could be paralyzed for ever they are bound to become fearful.

One of the standard tricks that stage hypnotists perform on their audience at the start of a show is to ask them to clasp their hands together. The hypnotist confidently claims that they won't be able to release their hands. What happens is that our knuckles naturally lock and create a bit of resistance when we try to unclasp our hands—but of course we can pull harder and release them. Some people, on feeling that first bit of resistance, say to themselves, 'It's true. I can't release my grip. I am hypnotized,' and auto-suggestion takes over from there. These are the people the hypnotist picks for his guinea pigs—he knows they will respond best to his suggestions. Thoughts about paralysis are like this too. If we say, 'I am paralyzed. This won't stop,' we can overreact a lot and convince ourselves that the feelings of paralysis will go on forever. But as with most of the strange feelings associated with panic they do pass, without any physical harm at all.

Myth No. 8: 'I will choke'

As mentioned in Chapter 4, there are certain physical changes to the throat and mouth occurring during panic attacks, which are part of the body's normal 'fear reaction'. Muscle tension plays a big part in feelings of choking. None of these changes is dangerous. Though they can give the impression that the sufferer might die, muscles cannot possibly constrict to the point of choking a person to death.

Sometimes the sufferer tries to compensate to avoid choking

by eating food slowly and swallowing very carefully. Some people eat only 'sloppy' food, avoiding meat, nuts or anything that might get stuck in the throat. Unfortunately these 'compensations' change something quite automatic into a controlled and thought-about activity. This tends to destroy the natural rhythmn of the body, making the person more likely to choke than if they ignored the problem.

Myth No. 9: 'I can't swallow'

During a panic attack the sufferer may focus on the changes to swallowing that are part of the fear reaction—as mentioned earlier, not much saliva is produced in the mouth or throat during fear, which makes the mouth go dry and gives rise to difficulty in swallowing. The sufferer may become frightened that their swallowing will be permanently impaired or that they won't be able to swallow food. Some compensate by doing a test every few minutes—swallowing just to check that it works. Again, this destroys the natural rhythm of the body and makes it more painful and difficult to swallow. This is not dangerous, but makes eating uncomfortable.

Myth No. 10: 'I can't breathe'

In fear and panic the body is trying to take in more oxygen, so naturally there will be changes to the sufferer's breathing, such as breathing faster. People may start to focus on these changes and become afraid about their breathing. They may feel that they can't get enough air in, or that they may overbreathe and cause themselves harm, or that their breathing will stop altogether. They may feel they have to keep a careful watch over their breathing or make sure they are breathing in enough air. All this puts a perfectly normal and automatic bodily function under voluntary control, and fear itself increases the breathing rate. Breathing works best when ignored and left to its own devices. The body is amazing in keeping the perfect balance of oxygen/carbon dioxide in the blood.

8

Mental Myths

Myth No. 11: The depths of black madness?

People are often afraid of losing control and going mad during a panic attack. One patient put it like this:

'The fear is that I am going crazy, I am going mad, that this is going to be the worst attack I ever had. And that this attack is going to be so bad that I can never recover from it, and I will have a complete, uh, just lunge into the depths of black madness, you know, from which there is no recall. And I am taking very short, rapid breaths. I am breathing like that and you know the world is closing in on me, and this is the end, you know, there is no way out. I just want to run and get the hell out of there.'[13]

As panic gets stronger and especially if feelings such as feeling disconnected from one's body, confused, or unreal occur, people may assume this is the start of madness, and of course they will fight hard to stop themselves entering an overpowering insanity that seems to be sucking them in for ever.

Psychiatrists have for many years distinguished major mental illness—the 'psychoses' (such as schizophrenia and manic depression) from the 'neuroses', which are basically anxiety conditions. (The term 'neurosis' is now rather old-fashioned. It suggests an illness—which panic is certainly not. It is also used in the negative sense of a 'neurotic person' which is unhelpful.) But whatever phrase we use, anxiety conditions are different from major mental illness. In anxiety, basically the sufferer is absolutely normal, although there is a pocket of experience and emotion that they cannot control in the way they would like to. This is not connected with psychotic mental illness which involves major changes in thinking and behaviour, such as hallucinations, delusions of grandeur or of being persecuted, or the inability to think logically.

The many people who have allowed a panic attack to run its course without trying to reduce or stop it have found that although they temporarily lose their usual grip on their emotional life, the feelings soon right themselves and they are left unscathed and perfectly sane—like the emotional release of crying mentioned in Chapter 5. *Fear* of mental illness, or fear of losing control of their thinking and judgment, rather than mental illness itself, is the problem. A panic attack does not propel someone into mental illness. It is not a sign of mental illness, or the start of mental illness. It is an emotional rather than a mental problem.

Myth No. 12: 'I'm out of control'

The common factor in this group of myths is that the person will lose control of certain bodily functions, or of their judgment, and do something awful or embarrassing.

'I will do something foolish—start to babble, scream, vomit, wet myself, or in some way socially embarrass myself.'

Some people are very conscious of how they may appear and what others may think of them during a panic attack; what stupid and embarrassing things they might do. The sufferer assumes the whole world must notice them because the sensations feel so strong. However, most people in the streets or at work are so busy leading their own lives and doing their own thing that they are not really aware of others.

It is rather like having an ulcer in your mouth. It feels enormous until you look at it in the mirror, and then you see it is the size of a pin-head. The fact that feelings are so strong does not mean that they are strong or important to others, or that it is obvious in the way one looks.

Some sufferers happen to catch sight of themselves during a panic in a mirror or shop window and are thoroughly amazed at how normal they look. They aren't that interesting to the average woman or man in the street, scrambling to do the shopping last thing before the shops close, or agitated by the children squabbling. Even if passers-by notice something, such as a reddening of the person's face, they are more likely to make sense of it by saying to themselves something like, 'That person looks hot,' or 'I wonder if they have high blood pressure'—that is, if they even notice.

Some people think that they will somehow lose control of their bodily functions and wet themselves, or vomit, as their feelings become stronger. Others imagine that their speech will become scrambled and they will speak gibberish. Others have a mental picture of themselves reaching such a pitch that they run around screaming, berserk, out of control, bumping into people and things thoroughly making a fool of themselves, with people staring at them all the while. Still others picture themselves losing control of their reason and having no more control of their actions, entering a nightmare world in which they have completely lost control of themselves and become as helpless as a baby.

These are tricks of feeling and imagination. They do not actually occur. It is important to distinguish feelings of losing control with actually losing control of one's actions. In the human body, feelings and actions have two different parts of the nervous system devoted to them—the autonomic part (feelings) and the skeletal muscles (actions). The two operate completely differently. People don't have so much control over what they feel, but they do have control of their actions, even though their mind may trick them into thinking, 'You will lose control.'

VOMITING

'Whenever I got close to a shop, even the thought about going into it, I started to feel hot with a horrible nauseous feeling and I thought, I can't go in. I just couldn't risk being sick in front of all those people.'

I have occasionally heard patients say to me that they worried so much about something that they did actually vomit. The feelings of increasing nausea that some people experience during panic easily leads them to think that they might vomit, which would be terribly embarrassing.

Much of what was said about passing out applies here. Has the person really vomited in the past? Was there some accidental cause in the past connected with panic, such as food poisoning? Most people with this fear do not actually vomit when they put themselves to the test and allow themselves to go through a panic. However, a few people do report that they are actually sick through fear. Sometimes they make themselves sick in order to get it over with, through fear that they might be sick! Sometimes the so-called 'vomiting' is only regurgitation of food. For those people whose major symptom during a panic attack is nausea, it is very unlikely that they will vomit, but it is an outside possibility.

GOING TO THE TOILET

'When I was going anywhere I found that as long as I knew where the toilet was I could manage fine. But I hit real problems when I had to go somewhere new. I'd be thinking all the time, "What if I can't find a toilet in time?" and in no time at all I'd feel really desperate for the loo.'

Wetting oneself is another type of socially embarrassing fear; as panic surges the most noticeable thing for some people is the strong desire to go to the toilet. The obvious fear to occur to them is, 'Supposing I was to wet myself? That would be dreadful.' The thought becomes almost a certainty in the person's imagination.

However, despite strong sensations in the bowel and bladder, people do not wet themselves or defecate during panic. Most people have learnt terrific control over their bladders from childhood upwards; if our control was really so poor, how is it that, as adults, we can control our bladders even during the deepest of sleeps? Why should this all change so that we wet ourselves when afraid?

HARMING OTHERS

'In the evening I would get home from work and do all the usual things . . . you know, have tea, watch the telly, but sometimes this panic feeling just crept up on me and straight away I'd be up and out of there. I'd get in the car and drive and drive till I felt it was safe.'

This man was afraid that if he had a panic in his house he would do harm to his wife. That was his firm belief. Some panic sufferers are afraid that the feelings will mount to such terrible heights that they will lose their control over themselves and kill or injure their loved ones, or other people, or themselves; or not know what they are doing and walk into a bus, or jump out of a moving train. They have misunderstood lack of control; they think that because they can't control their emotions in the way that they would like, they will not be able to control their actions. But the two are quite different. People do not harm those they love during panic. Their emotions may seem to go haywire but sufferers always retain control over their actions. If someone is worried that they might injure others, it suggests they don't really want to do it. Worry or fear is the problem, not that they will really attack or injure their loved ones.

A paper tiger?

In the last four chapters we have looked at many of the common fears that people have during a panic attack. Any of these fears, or combination of fears, is perfectly reasonable if people have sudden and unbearable feelings that they haven't experienced before. I think anyone could jump to the same conclusions if they experienced the sudden, unexplained, powerful feelings which make up a panic attack. But, even though these explanations involving fear of various disasters, physical and mental, are reasonable and logical enough to explain the feelings, they are simply wrong. Sufferers are not mad or stupid to think these things. It's just that they have misunderstood what panic feelings are. In fact, a panic attack cannot mentally or physically harm the sufferer in any way at all. It really is safe—like a deadly-looking snake which is in fact quite harmless. No poison. No bite.

Why is it, though, that one person fears one thing during panic and someone else fears something completely different? The panic feelings are pretty much the same for both people but one may fear that a panic is a heart attack, whereas the other may fear it is mental illness. Why don't they fear the same thing?

One man I saw for treatment of panics could not understand why he should fear that he would stop breathing, pass out and die during panic. On learning his story, though, it was clear to me that the idea of illness, death, and breathing problems was a strong one in his family. When younger he remembered his brother with bronchitis struggling for air during the night and believing that at any time he might die. His father had died of pneumonia. He had recently witnessed a cousin have a very disturbing asthma attack in which she could not breathe properly and went blue in the face; he himself was rather overweight and puffed and panted under exertion. His connection with illness and breathing problems was clear, and it was not hard to see why when he first experienced a panic attack he immediately thought 'I won't get enough air—I'll die.'

Other patients have seen relatives die of heart attacks, or have always had a secret fear of mental illness. There may have been an aunt who was mentally ill—and all the family say, 'Oh, aren't you like Auntie Elizabeth!' This sort of experience can often influence a person's ideas about panic attacks. Alternatively, sometimes a certain feeling that is very strong, such as a fast-beating heart, can naturally suggest to the person a heart problem rather than being related to any past experiences.

For whatever reason, one person can fear one thing about a panic attack and another can fear something completely different. The only thing the two explanations have in common is that they are fears of some disaster happening. We could even say the person has come to believe in a lie, or that their feelings have tricked them into believing that they are in danger.

Is panic all in the mind? No, not at all. The physical sensations are there all right. But the idea of what might happen during panic is in the mind—in the imagination.

PART III

Root Causes

9

What Causes Panic?

When panic attacks first occur they are often out of the blue, spontaneous, with no obvious reason. The person didn't do anything unusual on the day they occurred and didn't seem to be under more stress than usual. It seems a complete mystery why suddenly panic strikes. Even after panic has unfortunately become part of someone's lifestyle, they may still be puzzled as to why panic attacks occur on some days and not others.

The invisible cord

Although a sufferer may see no obvious reason for the first panic attacks, there is usually a connection with events in that person's life. The person may miss the connection entirely, which is why I call it an invisible cord. However, the connection is there. Probably the reason for this failure to connect events is that the person is looking in the wrong place. Usually when we experience very strong sensations we look around us to see what is causing it at that moment. Is something threatening me? Am I in danger? Have I got a dangerous illness? Or we may connect panic with what has happened in the last hour or two. What did I eat? Was I poisoned? Have I caught a terrible virus? Sufferers rarely look further back than a day to explain their panic attacks. This is why they fail to make the correct connection—they are using the wrong time-frame.

Sufferers should not look for a connection in terms of what has been happening in that hour, that day or even that week. They should be looking at the events of the previous one to nine months. It's not the close-up shot that counts—they need to put the zoom lens on, and look into the middle distance. Most patients I see, when asked if there was anything important going on in their lives at the time of their first panic attack, will say 'no'; but as they describe the months before that first panic they report all kinds of events—parents dying, a marriage breaking up, a severe car crash or an operation. To the outside observer it is obvious they have been under stress, but because the panic attack did not occur at exactly the same time as the stressful event, the connection escapes them.

What's your stress?

There are many studies which show that in the months before the first unexpected panic attack the sufferer had been going through a period of stress or trauma, or several things had happened which heaped up on top of each other. Here are some of the common stresses:

▶ death or illness of partner, close relative, friend

▶ illness/operation or disability of partner

▶ marriage problems—separation, arguments, return after a period of separation, violent or very critical partner, self or partner having an affair, divorce proceedings

▶ children—having a baby, miscarriage or stillbirth or abortion, illness/accident with children, grown-up child leaves home, pressure of looking after a young family

▶ family—having to look after an ageing parent, over-control or meddling from parents in your life

▶ moving away from home, starting a new job, college course, moving to a new house or new area

▶ your own physical health—an operation, illness, disability, menopause

- ► disasters/accidents—being in a car crash or accident, seeing others hurt (for example, just missed by a speeding car)

- ► work—too much stress at work, deadlines, more responsibility, long hours without breaks, boredom, bad atmosphere at work, failure to get promotion, too many hassles on job, redundancy, threats of redundancy, retirement

- ► business failure, money worries, mortgage problems

- ► effect of taking illegal drugs or legal medicines (as many as 10 per cent of initial panic attacks are set off by taking drugs; see for example the personal account of a GP whose first panic was set off by smoking marijuana as a student[22])

- ► after an illness or virus.

Some of the less tangible causes of stress researchers have drawn attention to are:

- ► separation experiences, such as leaving home for the first time, separation by partner dying, moving away from home and friends

- ► being trapped, for example in an unhappy marriage or an overstressful job, or having to live with in-laws

- ► losing control of important parts of your life, for instance your job, your social life

- ► being controlled by a parent/partner.

Almost any of the above stresses may be enough to set the scene for panic happening. Often one problem on its own is not enough, but two or three problems can pile up to create 'system overload'.

But why did the panic strike just then?

A common reaction to this idea is, 'OK, if there was a period of stress in my life over months, why did the panic strike on 3 June? Why not a day earlier or later? Why not 1 May?'

LOWERED RESISTANCE

One researcher[23] carried out a survey of panic sufferers and found that one or more of the long list of stresses described above occurred in the few months before panic attacks first happened. He also discovered that for 60 per cent of the sufferers he studied there was a period of lowered resistance just before the first panic attacks occurred. This included:

▶ delayed air flight causing exhaustion

▶ menopausal flushing

▶ irregular period

▶ inner ear inflammation

▶ flu.

The birth of a child is also a common time when a woman's physical and emotional stamina is low and she is made more vulnerable.

RELAXING

Another odd thing, which often throws the person completely off the scent, is that the first panic attacks may occur during a time of relaxation, a long-awaited holiday, or after a bad period of stress is over. It is as if the stress has been building up—then the person relaxes and bang! panic strikes.

A LITTLE TRIGGER

Apart from the 'background' causes of panic there is often a trigger, the last straw that broke the camel's back. For instance, one man who had all his life tried to help and assist his family was cheated and hurt by nearly every family member in turn, eventually being cheated out of the family inheritance. His pent-up hurt and anger about the way he was treated was the background cause of his panic. The 'trigger' for his first panic attack was a silly little incident—a fuse blowing with a bang.

Figure 6 shows how panic is set off.

Fig. 6: How panic attacks start

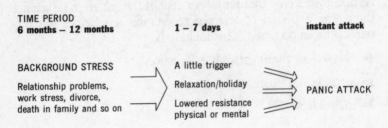

TIME PERIOD
6 months – 12 months   **1 – 7 days**   **instant attack**

BACKGROUND STRESS   A little trigger

Relationship problems,   Relaxation/holiday
work stress, divorce,   PANIC ATTACK
death in family and so on   Lowered resistance
physical or mental

The results of panic

I have tried to explain some of the reasons why a panic attack
first occurs, but the sufferer may be just as confused about why
panic should continue so long (often many years) after the first
few attacks. After a few panic attacks the sufferer begins to
predict when or where they might occur again or what seems to
set them off.

Chapter 3 explains how panic begins to change people—fear
of more attacks gives them an inner focus in which they are
hypersensitive to the first sensations of panic. The fear of these
sensations sets up a vicious cycle: fear produces more sensations
which produces more fear which produces more sensations
which produces more fear and so on. The reason sufferers fear
having another panic attack is the damage they think it might do
to them—maybe causing a heart attack, fainting or madness.

To stop these unpleasant consequences, the sufferer begins to
avoid places, situations, feelings, fixed plans, actions, certain
thoughts—even dropping off to sleep. So much mental energy
goes into avoiding these things that bit by bit the their lifestyle
changes. And they usually don't like the person they've now
become.

Two causes for panic

Coming back to my original point, there is an invisible world of connections of which panic sufferers are only vaguely aware. They usually don't realize the first panic is caused by stressful events in their life—difficulties or troubles that may have started months before the panic. In the few days before the first panic there may have been a period of lowered resistance, a 'trigger' event or a period of relaxation which set the scene for the panic to occur.

When the panic occurs the person does not connect it with the background causes but (not unreasonably) puts it down to other causes: heart attack, nervous breakdown, brain tumour.

The last piece in the jigsaw is that once a sufferer begins to be afraid of the sensations they get in panic, fear of the sensations can keep the panic reaction going, often over years.

This means there are really two main causes for panic:

▶ the original background cause for the first panic attacks

▶ after the first panics, fear of more panic attacks.

This is important in guiding therapy, as we will see in the next chapter.

10

Dealing with the Root Causes

I have a colleague at the Department of Psychology in Aberdeen who, in treating panic sufferers, always focuses on the fear of panic sensations first, and then if there is some emotional causes will explore these later. I tend to work the other way round. We each know the other does it the wrong way round! Actually, neither of us has any proof that one way is better than the other but, since you're stuck with me, let's look at the emotional causes first.

The last chapter explained that there were two sides to panic. In therapy we need, therefore, to cater for two different types of sufferer:

▶ the person who has not solved the original background cause for panics and is also struggling with the fear of panic attacks. This person will need a two-pronged attack aimed at helping them to unravel the background causes and overcome their fear of panic.

▶ the person who long ago got over or resolved the original cause of panic attack (for example, the death of a parent) and is now faced with just the fear of panic. Actually, 'just' is completely the wrong word, because fear is such a wretched experience that it can ruin lives. Fear of panic can keep panic alive even after the original cause has long disappeared. In this second case we need not focus on the original causes at all.

A sufferer shouldn't, however, make assumptions like, 'It was five years ago my husband died and therefore I must have resolved it by now.' If someone does not grieve, talk about or work through the painful experience that set panic off in the first place, but pushes it to the background, it remains like a land-mine—buried in the ground but still capable of detonating in the future. Time alone is not the measure of whether the cause has been dealt with.

Can sufferers tell which of the two types they are?

The only guideline here is that if panic attacks are new in a person's life, the causes are probably still active. If the panics started years ago, the causes may have disappeared in the mists of time—though not necessarily. I would advise going through the set of exercises in this chapter anyway.

Is it possible for people to find out the causes themselves?

There are problems which hinder people from identifying causes. Some of these are:

▶ the cause is not connected in time to the panic attack so doesn't seem to be involved

▶ the cause doesn't seem important enough to set off such a massively strong attack

▶ the sufferer has difficulty accepting that events in their life can cause physical, bodily sensations

▶ the causes may be too painful to think about

▶ the sufferer may be afraid to think about upsetting events

▶ the sufferer may think that even if they put their finger on the cause there is nothing they can do about it, so it's best to pretend it's not there

▶ the person may subconsciously 'block off' the cause

▶ there may be several small causes that together add up, though each by itself seems too small to cause panic.

A seven-point programme for identifying the background causes of panic

Here is a step-by-step programme to help the panic sufferer identify what may have originally caused their panic. Sufferers should go through each step. They should be honest with themselves: on the one hand, they should not let me put ideas in their head; on the other hand, they should not ignore things or pretend they are unimportant.

It is quite common for people to push upsetting things to the back of their mind. It seems to hurt less that way. In these exercises I am asking them to do the reverse of that; to think about hurtful events. The problem with pushing things into the background is that they tend not to go away of their own accord, but stay put, to pop up later in the person's life in a way that is unwanted and doesn't make sense—for example, by causing panic attacks.

STEP 1: STARTING A WRITTEN LIST OF POSSIBLE CAUSES FOR THE FIRST PANIC

When did your first panic attack happen? Write down the date as accurately as possible.

Think back over the nine months before this. What was happening in your life? What had changed in your life, both good and bad? Make a written list of anything that you can remember, big and small.

Write first, and decide the causes later. Especially be sure to write down any 'forbidden' things you may usually push into the background because you don't want to think about them.

This example is of Katy, a 23-year-old girl living alone with her new baby.

<u>First panic:</u> May/June 1990, just after moving to my flat.

<u>Causes of panic:</u>
Moved into flat with Ryan (new baby).
Tried evening job as barmaid but babysitter fell through and had to give it up.
Stuck in flat with Ryan all day.

STEP 2: TOPPING UP YOUR LIST

As a further way to pinpoint anything you may have missed in Step 1, use the list of events on page 84 to help identify any other things that might have been important.

This covers some key stresses under the headings of relationships, children, work, friends and relatives, health, disaster and accidents, finance, home, crime and vocational training.

Katy's list now looked like this:

<u>Causes of panic:</u>
Moved into flat with Ryan (new baby).
Tried evening job as barmaid but babysitter fell through and had to give it up.
Stuck in flat with Ryan all day.
Loss of independence (not getting out of flat).
Had an affair.
Had serious argument with Mum.
Left home (one year ago).
Could not pay rent on flat.

STEP 3: YOUR REACTION TO THINGS ON THE LIST.

Look down your list. Does any of the events you have written down upset you, worry you, make you want to cry, depress you or generally 'get to you'? If one or more things does, underline them to remind you later that these might be important.

Katy wrote down her reaction to her list:

<u>Causes of panic:</u>
Moved into flat with Ryan (new baby)
<u>Tried evening job as barmaid but babysitter fell through and had to give it up.</u> *Depresses me.*
<u>Stuck in flat with Ryan all day.</u> *Worries me. I might have an attack and not be able to get help.*
Loss of independence (not getting out of flat).
<u>Had an affair.</u> *Makes me want to cry.*
<u>Had serious argument with Mum.</u> *Makes me angry.*
<u>Left home (one year ago).</u> *Also makes me angry.*
Could not pay rent on the flat.

STEP 4: SHARING WITH ANOTHER PERSON

Share what you have found with someone who knows you well and you can trust, either showing them what you have written or explaining it to them. Often other people can see what is staring us in the face that we have missed. It will probably help us to get our ideas in proportion.

This is what Katy did:

'I showed my list to the Health Visitor. We went through it together. She asked me why I was angry with my mother. I said that she had kicked me out of home when she found out I was pregnant but had started to visit not because of me, but because of Ryan. Then I started to cry for no good reason. She said this must be important for me to cry about it—but I still don't understand why it gets at me so much.

'Also she asked if I was upset about Ryan's father not living with me—not really. What will be will be.'

STEP 5: REVISING YOUR LIST

Write a new list changing the order of the events so that what you feel is most important is top of the list, then the second most important next and so on. Take into account what your friend has said (Step 4), what you have underlined (Step 3), and your 'gut feelings' about what is important.

Katy's revised list:

Causes of panic:
1 Had serious argument with Mum. *Gut feeling it's important but still don't know why.*
2 Left home (one year ago).
3= Tried evening job as barmaid but babysitter fell through and had to give it up.
3= Stuck in flat with Ryan all day.
3= Loss of independence (because of not getting out of flat) *Same as being stuck in flat.*
4 Had an affair.
5 Moved into flat with Ryan (new baby).
6 Could not pay rent.

STEP 6: PLANNING WHAT YOU COULD DO TO CHANGE THINGS

Write down opposite each cause things that you could possibly do to change the situation, help resolve it or make you feel better about it. Even if something, such as an assault, occurred in the past, there are still things that you can do, such as seek out a counsellor, friend or minister to talk it over with, cry, pour out your thoughts in writing or into a tape recorder, pray about it and/or initiate legal action (if not done already).

Katy's plans:

Causes of panic:
1 Had serious argument with Mum. *I have a gut feeling that this is really important but I still don't know why. I need to talk to the Health Visitor again.*
2 Leaving home (one year ago). *I don't know how to get rid of my anger. Is there some local women's group I could go to? I have a problem finding a babysitter.*
3= Tried evening job as barmaid but babysitter fell through and had to give it up.

Try to get another babysitter—money a problem. Join
babysitting circle?

3= Stuck in flat with Ryan all day. *Could go for walks in*
summer. Join group?

3= Loss of independence (because of not getting out of flat).
Same as being stuck in flat.

4 Had an affair. *I don't want to tell K____ that he's the*
father but I'd like him to know. No, I wouldn't. I don't
understand it.

5 Moved into flat with Ryan (new baby). *Can't change this.*

6 Could not pay rent. *Not a problem now.*

'I want to cry as I'm writing most of these answers. The
Health Visitor says I should cry a lot more. I did a bit when she
was here last. I feel I've got everything bottled up inside me
and it could explode and I couldn't cope. If I do cry I feel a bit
better but also it's scary because it feels like a panic attack
coming on. I think I should let myself cry a lot more. I realize I
try to block it each time I feel tears starting—I usually run
out the room and put the TV on or blast out a tape really loud
to drown out my feelings.'

STEP 7: TAKING ACTION

Actively take steps to change or carry out some of the actions
you have suggested in Step 6.

Some actions may be dramatic, such as changing jobs.
Obviously you would have to consider such an important
decision long and hard, maybe consulting friends or your
partner about it, or just 'sitting on it' for a while until it
becomes clearer. At other times a minor change may help a lot,
for example, taking breaks, pacing yourself better at work or
dropping the overtime. This sort of change can be put into action
as soon as possible.

In the example given in this chapter Katy does not fully
understand what has upset her so much. She probably needs to
have counselling to explore the events and her feelings more

fully. For some readers this chapter may help show them what the root causes for the original panic attacks were. For others, like Katy, it may only help to show up rough problem areas which they should follow up further by talking to a close friend or seeking professional help.

Table 1 Events which can lead up to the initial panic attack
Tick any event that occurred in 6 months before first panic attack.

Relationships
Got married
Trapped in a marriage
Unhappy relationship
Loss of independence
Had an affair
Separation or divorce from partner
Partner was physically violent or abusive
Serious illness or death of partner
Partner stopped work
A member of your family died
Serious argument with partner
Leaving home

Children
Birth of child
Death of child
Child gets married
Child leaves home
Illness in child
Serious argument with child
Partner treats child badly

Work
Overwork
Became unemployed
Retirement, or having to leave work
Increase in job responsibility
Too many hassles at work
Argument with boss or fellow worker
Change in job or type of work
Unhappy with job

Friends & Relations
Close friend moves away
Loss of friends
Family member moves into your
household
Having to look after invalid

Health
Start or worsening of illness
Had an operation
Miscarriage, stillbirth or abortion
Menopause

Disasters and Accidents
Was in car, train, boat or other accident
Was injured
Saw others badly hurt or killed
Nearly killed
Was in explosion, fire, nearly drowned

Finance
Not enough money
Could not pay loan/mortgage/rent
Fear of loss of home
Property loss
Took cut in wages
Financial loss
Repossession

Home
Moved to new house/flat
Moved to new area/country
Moved out of a home
Lost a home through fire, flood, other
disaster

Crime
Was attacked or threatened or bullied
Was sexually assaulted
Was robbed
Was involved in a fight
Had courtcase
Carried out an offence

College/training
Start at college/training
Final exams
Failed training
Difficulties with college authorities

PART IV

A Practical Therapy Programme for Panic

11

Attitude!

Chapters 11 to 15 describe a series of practical exercises for panic sufferers. They are part of the therapy, not the entire therapy programme. The information about panic attacks, as contained in Chapters 2 to 8, and the identification of causes for panic, in Chapters 9 to 10, are equally parts of overcoming panic. Chapters 11 to 15 provide the sufferer with a practical way of testing out the truth about panic for themselves. It is up to them whether they want or need this part of the therapy.

Before considering this practical side to therapy it is crucial to develop the right attitude of mind. Success hangs on this. The right attitude involves:

▶ how to handle good and bad days

▶ how to handle setbacks

▶ not expecting the miracle cure.

There will always be set-backs. Set-backs are normal. Therapy does not fail because of set-backs. It only fails if the person reacts in the wrong way to them. Let us look at some different attitudes to these practical exercises.

Good days and bad days

'Bad days' when depression and anxiety crowd in on a person are the single biggest threat to therapy. Good days and bad days are common in anxiety and panic. A person will have a day or a few days where things seem almost normal. Then, for no clear reason, those terrible feelings return again. Occasionally this bad spell may last more than a few days—more like a week.

Sufferers may not understand the reason for a bad day and this may worry them. Sometimes bad days are due to a period of change, stress or tiredness; sometimes to a physical illness like flu; sometimes it is pre-menstrual tension; and sometimes the person has stopped taking the right approach to fears and has gone back to old habits that make things worse. Sometimes there doesn't seem any good reason at all for a bad day.

BAD DAYS ARE NORMAL
Actually, when you think about it, good days and bad days are common to all humanity, but bad days don't signify anything too special for most people. They may be uncomfortable but people will not think twice about them. But for the panic sufferer a 'bad day' carries a whole different meaning. Sufferers seem to know almost from the point of waking up that this is a bad day—they feel tense and worked up all day, and are in dread of having a panic attack. There is also regret and annoyance when they seemed to be doing quite well and then one of these wretched bad days appeared; just like the 'friend' who has the habit of arriving on your doorstep for a chat just at the wrong time. It is important for the sufferer to learn to accept that good days and bad days are normal; not to get too excited about good days, nor too down about bad.

BACK TO SQUARE ONE
Let us suppose a sufferer has started the therapy programme and has made tremendous strides in overcoming panic; they have just had a week without any panic feelings at all when suddenly a full-blown panic attack occurs. The most usual thought that goes through the sufferer's mind is, 'Oh no. I'm back to square one again. This programme is not working. What's the point in carrying on?'

But on bad days like this they should not say 'back to square one'; but something like, 'I've made progress before, I can do it again.'

YOU CAN'T LEARN ANYTHING NEW WITHOUT THE ODD FAILURE

It is rather like learning to ride a bike for the first time. It comes gradually. If the first time learners fall off they say, 'It's not working—I'll never learn this,' they may give up and never learn at all. They must realize that set-backs are part of the learning process, dust themselves off and get back onto the bike again.

Before this part of therapy starts, sufferers should settle it in their minds that set-backs are normal and should be expected, and work out how they will handle them when rather than if they occur.

THE COURSE OF THERAPY NEVER RUNS SMOOTH

Progress in therapy will not be even. Figure 7 (see page opposite) shows what normally happens. It is a picture of what happens when a panic sufferer begins to improve—for instance, if someone was following the self-help instructions in this book or seeing a clinical psychologist for help.

The downward line shows improvement over a six- to nine-month period. But as we can see the improvement is not at all even—there are many ups and downs from day to day though at the end of therapy panic has disappeared. Look at point A on the graph—let us say that is a Monday—very little anxiety all day. Tuesday (point B) is a bad day—'What's happening? Oh no, back to square one.' The sufferer feels demoralization and despair, and feels like giving up. But it is not back to square one, it is only part of the random ups and downs of the body. Overall the person is improving, but they cannot see this from one day to another. Panic sufferers should take a long-term view of therapy. They must not be swayed by a bad day or a bad week.

THE GOOD SHOWS UP THE BAD

As a person gets better they notice bad days more. Let's say at the beginning of therapy someone has panics every second day. Then they begin to improve and have five full days free of panic. They start to feel that life is worth living again and begin to have hope that they really can buck it this time. Then on the sixth day they have a panic attack. All the old gloom comes back and they can hardly be blamed for thinking, 'It's all an illusion. I can never change.' But this is based on an underlying mistaken belief. We might call it 'the overnight miracle cure attitude'—the idea that our problem must immediately disappear 100 per cent and never appear again. Actually, as therapy goes on, the bad days stand out more in comparison with the good days.

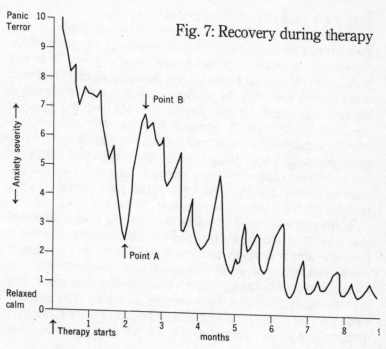

Fig. 7: Recovery during therapy

TO BE A LONG-DISTANCE RUNNER

The point is that a person must take a long-term view of therapy. They *can* change. So on a bad day the sufferer should:

▶ realize it is only a temporary set-back

▶ not give up hope. Remember the improvement they have made and that good times are possible again.

▶ realize that if they carry on with what was successful before, they will win through and be successful again.

The three buts

There are three quite common reasons why people will not try therapy:

BUT I'VE HAD IT FOR TOO LONG

If someone has suffered for many years it is understandable that they should feel this. But it doesn't matter if the problem has been with someone two months or twenty years; it is still possible to change. One major book on agoraphobia[24] reviewed what factors were able to predict which sufferers improved in therapy and which did not. They concluded that 'the therapist need not be daunted by patients who are very anxious, are slightly depressed or have phobias of considerable severity or great duration... surprising results can be achieved with even the most handicapped or disadvantaged patients'. I know of at least one lady who suffered from panic and agoraphobia for twenty-five years but has overcome it.

If anxiety has been with a person for so long I can understand that hope long ago went out of the window. Sufferers feel better for a day and at first say to themselves, 'It's gone!—but then it comes back again, time and time again, until they despair of ever finding a cure. For some, anxiety is so familiar that when they start to recover they feel really strange, as if they were missing some familiar companion, and almost look around for something to worry about. No one can give a 100 per cent promise of full recovery, but with correct information and understanding and by using the right approach there is a good chance of overcoming panic anxiety.

BUT THE FEELINGS ARE SO CRIPPLING
One of the hallmarks of panic attacks is that the sensations people experience are so very powerful and seem to increase dramatically once they start. This can become so bad as to make it difficult for them to concentrate or to carry out some of the simplest things in their life. However, when it comes to therapy for panic attacks it does not seem to make much difference how strong the sensations are, how many sensations the person experiences, or how frequently they have panic attacks. The same principles and good results seem to apply across the board. Recovery is not just limited to those with weak, infrequent or limited panic attacks.

BUT I'VE TRIED THIS BEFORE
Sometimes clients say this when this part of the therapy is explained. Yes, they have tried it before but they have tried a bit of this, a bit of that. A bit from this book. A magazine article recommends this, a friend suggested that. I once tried a relaxation tape, took pills for a bit. It's a bit like being tossed about by the waves—first in this direction, then in that.

What is needed is:

▶ determination—the person must keep going on, day after day, week after week. There will be set-backs, there will be failure. There should be no regrets, no despair, just a 'plodding on' attitude.

▶ right approach—of course, it is no use someone going on and on in the wrong direction; they end up miles from where they intended. The person must be sure that the direction and the programme is right for them—and then stick to it.

91

12

The Anatomy of Fear

Whether panic attacks were initially caused by being trapped in an unhappy marriage, the death of a child, leaving home or whatever reason, once the first panic attacks occur, fear usually steps in too.

When fear steps in

Sufferers become afraid of having more panic attacks, and afraid of what the attacks may mean. They are bewildered by what is happening to them. In this chapter I want to go on to examine the fear reaction in a bit more detail to help sufferers understand their fears about panic attacks better and find a way out of this vicious circle of fear. In fact, a sufferer may not have labelled their reaction to panics as 'fear'. They may call it 'discomfort' or 'anxiety', or may have been so successful in preventing panic attacks from occurring that they can't identify a fear at all.

Freezing the fear reaction

The fear reaction occurs in an instant so it is a bit difficult to see what is happening. Some video players have a button on the remote control panel which allows you to slow down a video film. We can slow down a film so much that it is possible to look at it frame by frame and observe details that would be impossible when viewing it in real time.

Let us suppose we could slow down the fear reaction like this. What would we find?

FREEZE FRAME 1

We would see that the very first part of the fear reaction does not involve the emotion of fear at all. The first part involves recognition.

The psychologists' jargon for this part of the reaction would be that the person first has to make an 'appraisal' of danger. In other words, before someone feels fear they must recognize that there is danger ahead. This is what 'appraising' danger means[25].

These 'appraisals' can be very simple sense recognitions involving little thought, such as seeing a snake or flames leaping around us.

These simple primitive types of danger seem to cause a reaction quite naturally in both animals and people. Another common 'automatic fear' provoker is loud noise. Great generals throughout the centuries have known this and instructed their troops to shout and scream when they attack the enemy.

Let's take a different illustration; suppose we are walking down a dark alley in the inner city late at night and at the end of the passage suddenly we see the silhouettes of two men appear. When they see us they stand perfectly still, waiting at the end of the passage.

Our 'appraisal' involves quite a high level of mental activity. It is based on the knowledge that late at night in cities, where there is little help available and under the cloak of darkness, crimes are committed. And that a person standing still at the end of a path means 'blocking your way'. And that two male figures who block your way in this place equal danger. Although this 'appraisal' may happen in an instant, it involves thoughts, knowledge and previous learning.

In other words, before our bodies register fear we must first recognize it. The recognition varies from simple recognition of naturally dangerous objects to thoughts and knowledge about what is dangerous.

FREEZE FRAME 2

The next part of the freeze frame concerns feelings or emotions of fear—all those feeling and sensations I talked about in Chapter 4: sweating, heart racing, breathlessness, tension, trembling, choking sensations, hot flushes, chest pain, nausea, dizziness, numbness and so on. As I explained in that chapter, these are a fairly standard set of very strong sensations designed to help us to react quickly to avoid danger. The reactions occur quite automatically when we are faced with danger and are common to everyone. Once danger is recognised or 'appraised' (freeze frame 1) the fear emotions are automatically 'switched on' (freeze frame 2).

FREEZE FRAME 3

The third part of the reaction is the way in which we respond. The strong sensations of fear produce a response in us. The most common natural response is to run, to fight, or to freeze. We can, however, learn to change our response to fear. I recently heard a story on the radio in which a twelve-year-old boy was interviewed. He had been attacked by a grizzly bear in the Rockies. He described the bear hitting and clawing him; then he went limp and pretended to be dead. He had heard some trappers a few days before saying that bears stop attacking someone once they think they are dead. He lay still, and the bear did go away. This is a case in which the boy felt all the fear emotions (freeze frame 2) which naturally made him want to run away but because of his 'inside knowledge' about bears he overrode the feelings and lay completely still. He was controlling his reaction to fear emotions.

Figure 8 shows the three main parts of the fear reaction.

1 $\rightarrow$	2 $\rightarrow$	3
Appraisal	**Fear emotions**	**Response**
Person registers danger	Person instantly feels strong bodily sensations	Person takes action such as running away, fighting

Drawing the reaction like this is rather artificial; we have slowed the frames down so much in order to take a look at the different parts of fear. In real life the whole fear reaction is so quick that it seems as if all the different parts of the reaction are rolled into one.

It's the thought that counts

Now here is an interesting and important part of this. Having fear emotions depends on whether we believe danger to exist. If we do not think danger exists our body will not react with fear at all. On the other hand, if we think danger exists, even though it doesn't, our bodies will react exactly the same way as if danger was really there. It all depends on our appraisal of danger.

Here are some examples of different sorts of appraisal:

▶ appraisal of danger when it is really there (Figure 9)

▶ failure to appraise danger when it is really there (Figure 10)

▶ appraisal of danger when it is not really there (Figure 11).

Fig. 9: Appraisal of danger when it is *really* there

Appraisal	Fear emotions	Reaction	Result
'There are 2 men waiting for me at the end of this dark passageway. This is midnight in the Bronx.'			
DANGER ⟹	Fear emotions experienced ⟹	Run fast in the opposite direction ⟹	You live to face another day

Fig. 10: *Failure* to appraise danger when it is *really* there

Appraisal	Fear emotions	Reaction	Result
'These 2 men waiting for me must be my 2 pals who said they'd be there'			

NO DANGER $\Rightarrow$ No fear emotions experienced $\Rightarrow$ Carry on walking towards the men $\Rightarrow$ Death through stabbing

Fig. 11: Appraisal of danger when it is *not really there*

Appraisal	Fear emotions	Reaction	Result
'There are 2 men waiting for me at the end of this passage.'			

DANGER $\Rightarrow$ Fear emotions experienced $\Rightarrow$ Run fast in the opposite direction $\Rightarrow$ You live to face another day, but don't discover the 2 'men' were a couple of stray cats sitting on top of some dustbins

Now let us look at a list of things that most people typically appraise as dangerous (Table 2) and compare it with the list typical of panic sufferers (Table 3). What is the difference between the two lists?

Table 2
Things which many people appraise as dangerous

Things which many people appraise as dangerous	Result feared
Threatening gang with knives	Knife wounds
Lions, tigers, bears, sharks on the loose	Mutilation or death
Your car goes into a skid	Injury, death
Snakes, scorpions, deadly spiders close by	Poisonous bites
Trapped in a fire	Burns
Experiencing a storm, hurricane, earthquake	Injury
Caught in a current when swimming	Drowning
Crowd on the rampage	Trampling to death
Sudden, severe pain	Serious illness

Table 3
Things (as well as the above) which panic sufferers 'appraise' as dangerous

Things (as well as the above) which panic sufferers 'appraise' as dangerous	Result feared
Palpitations	Impending heart attack
Dizziness	Losing consciousness
Being short of breath	Not being able to get enough air
Feelings of unreality	Losing control of the mind
Numbness	Passing out
Strong feelings in bladder	Wetting self
Feelings of paralysis	Impending death

What is dangerous to most people lies outside themselves—something 'out there' that may harm and kill them. For the panic sufferer, what is dangerous to them is inside them—feelings and sensations. When bodily sensations signal danger a person looks out for them all the time (the inner focus)—scanning the body for signs of danger. And, of course, many times throughout the day such bodily changes will be experienced. This means that the panic sufferer may be appraising danger several times every day and experiencing fear emotions each time. This is like living in a kind of perpetual hell of fear.

Mistaken danger

The panic sufferer definitely falls into the third category about appraisal. They are appraising danger when there is really no danger present. In other words, they will have the same reaction as anyone else when confronted by a thug with a knife. There is nothing wrong with the panic sufferer's emotional reaction—it is all in perfect working order. The only thing wrong is that they also mistakenly think danger will occur when none is present.

Please pause for a moment to see what this means. It is saying that panic sufferers are normal individuals. There is nothing wrong with their mental apparatus. They are emotionally responding to danger as they ought to be. There is no question of mental illness, instability or insanity. They are normal people who quite simply made a mistake. They believe that if a panic attack was left unchecked, some personal danger would happen to them. Anyone who believed what they believe would respond with the same fear reaction.

The problem lies with their mistaken appraisal or belief. The solution lies with the discovery that panic attacks are quite safe.

Focusing therapy

What part of the fear reaction should therapy attempt to change? If we tried to change the fear emotions (freeze frame 2) this might be harmful to the person; the next time danger arose the person might not react strongly enough to evade it. It would be possible to change reaction to the fear emotions (freeze frame 3) as the boy did with the grizzly bear. But even if sufferers changed their reaction they would still experience unpleasant fear emotions. The Cognitive Invalidation approach aims at changing the mistaken appraisal about the danger of panic attacks (freeze frame 1). When the person knows that panic is safe they will no longer experience fear emotions as they did before.

13

Taking the Sting out of Fear

How can a person discover that panic attacks, though unpleasant, are safe? Would it be by asking others who have had panic attacks? Would it be by talking it over with a friend? Would it be by listening to a therapist, or an expert on the TV or radio? Sometimes sufferers may hear from others that panic is safe and pay lip-service to this, but deep down they are unconvinced.

Getting at the deep-down belief

What needs to change is that deep-down belief or appraisal. Deep down, the panic sufferer fears that if a panic attack happened and was left to continue unchecked something terrible might happen.

They may not be able to put their finger on what that something might be, but it's pretty bad. It may include dying, going insane, losing control of mind and body. Deep down it's a real possibility and it's nasty.

How can one get at these deep-seated appraisals? You can't easily argue with yourself and force yourself to believe otherwise. Belief isn't so easily persuaded by such reasoning exercises. The best way to discover the truth of what really happens is by personal experience; sufferers need to discover the facts for themselves. They need to set up a personal 'experiment' to test out for themselves whether their belief is true[2, 3].

The personal experiment

If scientists set up an experiment they will design it in such a way as to test out their theory; the results of the study will either disprove or confirm their theory. If they said, 'I know the answer already so there's no need to test it out,' others would say, 'Prove it.' If they arranged an experiment which could only show their theory was right this would not be a proper test—it's rather like tossing a two-headed coin, which must come down heads. The experiment must be capable of disproving or proving the theory being tested.

What about the personal experiment? This too is set up to confirm or disprove something meaningful from the everyday life of an individual person. Panic sufferers can set up an experiment to test out what happens to them when a panic attack is left unchecked.

Entering the unknown

A sufferer may say at this point, 'But I've been through panic a thousand times. I know what will happen.' However, the sufferer is more like a scientist who has never properly tested the theory. Here are some of the things which may hold back that crucial experiment:

▶ they remember back to the first few terrible panic attacks they had, which seem to be seared into memory, and are so fixed on these attacks that it is difficult to shift to the present, and what would happen today

▶ the fear of what *might* happen is so strong that they assume it *will* happen. This, though, is an assumption, not a proven fact.

▶ because the feelings of panic are so unpleasant they have concentrated on the feelings and not stopped to consider what actually happens

▶ they have avoided places, situations, actions, feelings for a long time or used 'safety routines' to stop panic starting. So they have effectively blocked themselves off from the crucial question: what would happen without all these precautions?

▶ Their 'life-savers' which stop panic rising (deep breathing, relaxation, alcohol and so on) never allow panic to reach a natural peak, and so they never discover what would have happened otherwise.

This is how one sufferer explained how carefully every aspect of her life was planned so she could avoid anything that might set off a panic:

'I only know that I have been planning like this for many years, to such an extent that it has become part of my life. I am an expert at it. I am superb at thinking on my feet, at tremendous speed, and at telling white lies and making plausible excuses. I am sure that no one involved in my planning has the least idea that they are being constantly manipulated. I don't like the effort involved. The brain power it takes could be so much better used. The thing is, that if I just let happen what will, then I am entering the unknown.'

MRS F.A.

In order to carry out a proper test of what happens the sufferer needs to enter this 'unknown', and that requires tremendous resolve, courage and a bit of planning.

TERRY'S EXPERIMENT
To get the feel of what a personal experiment is like, let's take the example of Terry, a successful Dundee farmer who avoided going into shops and wouldn't visit anything more than a small town through fear of panic. Terry was fed up with the restrictions his panic imposed upon his life and was sure that it cost him a great deal financially. His case is an example where a single simple personal experiment was the key to his recovery. Many cases are not as straightforward and require a series of personal experiments, each one aimed at testing out a different aspect of the person's fear.

I saw Terry first after he had been referred by his GP for psychological therapy. In our first session he explained his fears and how they had developed over five years. His life had been getting more and more restricted as a result of his fear. His greatest fear was C & A's store in Aberdeen. In the second session I explained the nature of panic to him and how it was essential to find out what really happened. Rather than gradually approach his problem he wanted to 'go for gold' and carry out his personal experiment on the worst fear.

We both went into Aberdeen city centre. I parked my car, and after further 'briefing' we both walked into C & A. At first he walked quite quickly round the store looking intently at everything.

I asked why he seemed to be reading every label. 'To keep my mind off the panic,' he replied—this was his safety routine. I asked him not to distract his mind like this. He carried this out but still walked round quickly. 'Why are you moving around so fast?' I asked. 'It helps me not to feel dizzy feelings,' said Terry. I asked him if he would stand still. He agreed to stand in one spot. He stood, legs straddled, bracing himself. 'Why are you standing like that?' I again enquired. 'To stop myself falling over'—his ultimate fear. 'I'd like you to stand with your heels together,' I said.

This was the crunch point. I had asked him to do just about the hardest task possible. It was the crux of his experiment; the only way he could really test out whether he would fall down through panic. He reluctantly put his heels together. Immediately he did this a wave of panic came over him. But to his surprise he did not fall over, as expected, and the panic actually only lasted a few seconds. After this 'crunch' experience he started to go into many places and overcame most of his fear. He had been afraid to put the ultimate fear of falling over to the test and over the years had done everything possible to avoid this. Once he truly faced the thing he feared most, he discovered there was nothing really to be afraid of.

Setting up a personal experiment

Here are the steps a panic sufferer might follow to test out what really happens in a panic.

At the start the person needs to ask: 'What is the thing (or things) I am afraid might happen if I had a panic attack and didn't try to control it or stop it or escape from it in any sort of way?'

Some people find this difficult to answer. They may say that they are not afraid of anything happening. When I ask clients, 'What would happen if you didn't run out of the store when you had a panic attack?' they sometimes reply, 'But I would never let it get to that stage.' In other words, they have set up such an elaborate system of safety routines that they don't even have to think about what might happen. Sufferers should take away all their imaginary safety routines and say what is the worst they think could happen. Some of the most common beliefs about panic are covered in Chapters 5 to 8.

Having identified what they are afraid might happen they need to set up a series of personal experiments so as to discover whether this really does happen. The experiment would involve:

1 PUTTING THEMSELVES IN THE SITUATION THAT MIGHT SET OFF PANIC—NOT AVOIDING SITUATIONS

This may mean facing

▶ places

▶ situations

▶ feelings

▶ the anticipation of events

▶ actions

▶ thoughts about panic

▶ sleep.

2 NOT CARRYING OUT ANY ROUTINES LIKELY TO STOP A PANIC HAPPENING (SAFETY ROUTINES)

3 WHEN A PANIC STARTS, NOT DOING ANYTHING TO STOP IT REACHING ITS PEAK ('LIFE-SAVERS')

In other words, the person needs to allow a full-blown panic attack to occur. It is only after these steps 1, 2 and 3 have been taken that the person can truly discover what happens in a panic attack. When they discover by personal experience that they don't die, pass out, lose control and so forth, their fears and panicky feelings begin to be eroded. This type of experiment is, naturally, extremely threatening for a panic sufferer. It is asking them to risk their sanity or their life.

I mentioned that Terry's case was a simple single personal experiment. Before we go into any more detail let's get the feel of a more complex situation, in which Ralph needed to carry out a series of personal experiments in order to realize that panic was safe.

14

Ralph—an Example of Successful Therapy

The account of Ralph, a 28-year-old postgraduate student, is a true illustration of someone going through this therapy programme. He is an example of someone with very severe panic who completely recovered. Obviously everyone who experiences panic attacks is unique so no two people's cases will be exactly the same. Ralph's case has much in common with other panic sufferers but differs in certain features. One of the unusual aspects of his case was the age at which he first experienced panic attacks (thirteen years old). This is younger than is typically the case.

I first heard about Ralph when a psychiatrist at the hospital at which I worked asked me to see him as an urgent referral. He had been admitted voluntarily as an in-patient to one of the psychiatric wards, at the urgent request of his GP. The psychiatrist described him as intensely anxious, with a high pulse rate and profuse sweating. His stomach was churning and he had a fear of losing control of his bladder and bowel and of fainting. The psychiatrist started him on the drug fluoxetine, and decided to discharge him home with the idea of referring him to the Clinical Psychology Department to be seen as an out-patient (the most usual way panic sufferers are treated). However, Ralph returned to the ward the following day, having had a completely sleepless night with intense feelings of terror. He was given diazepam, along with fluoxetine, and the psychiatrist asked me to see him urgently.

Session 1: Fear of madness

I met Ralph first on the following day. This was to be the first of our thirteen sessions which altogether stretched over seven months. I asked him to describe what he had been experiencing recently. He felt that any problem in life could push him over the edge. Going 'over the edge' meant that he thought he might completely disintegrate, no longer being responsible for his actions, turning into a different person unable to return to normality. He also described a fear of breaking down in front of others—that he would start crying with no control over his emotions. In the last year his panic attacks had worsened. 'Now I would call them "terror attacks"', he told me.

He was completely bewildered about why he should be experiencing such terror—there was no particular cause that he could see, in fact he felt he had had quite a happy life in general. The fact that he saw no cause proved to him that he had an 'innate deficiency in my personality which can't be cured'. Going into a psychiatric hospital had simply confirmed his own worst fears about his insanity. He said while he was in hospital he experienced almost constant panic, feeling nothing could be done and that he could not cope. 'As if I would explode... I was rooted to the spot with fear.'

The point to realize here is that this man was experiencing severe tension, anxiety and fear. His problem was not insanity, but a fear of madness, and that fear stoked up more and more anxiety.

HOW IT ALL STARTED

I asked him to describe the problem right from the start. The idea at this point in therapy was to get him to put his thoughts in order and discover that there was a pattern and causes for his panic rather than it just being irrational. The sort of questions I asked were aimed at helping him to spot these causes and connections himself, just as described in chapters 9 and 10.

He remembered his earliest years as happy until the age of five, when his mother was admitted to hospital with a nervous breakdown. She was gone for a long time and he was given no explanation about it. His family moved about the world a lot. At the age of thirteen, when his family was living in Trinidad, he was sent to boarding school in the UK.

He arrived three days before term started. The whole school was empty and he slept in a large dormitory by himself. He was left alone the next day. There were no friends or relatives nearby. Over the next few days other pupils arrived with their parents, but from the start he felt he didn't fit in. The first panic attack was still vivid in his mind. He was sitting in the school hall with many boys round about him. Suddenly he experienced terrific fear and wanted to get out. He was confused because he could see no reason why he should suddenly and for no apparent reason be struck with such strong, overpowering emotion.

After this he began to be afraid of speaking in front of a group of boys, which he refused to do, and apprehensive of any new places. Eighteen months later he was moved to another boarding school nearer to relatives, where he felt less isolated, and the problem largely subsided.

At eighteen years old he went to Birmingham University to study economics. He lived with a friend in a nearby flat and this was quite a good period in his life, when he was reasonably clear of panic. After graduating at the age of twenty-one he set up in his own business, later moving to Cardiff to live closer to his father who had separated by then from his mother.

When he was twenty-five, the relationship with the woman he had lived with for six years broke up. At this point he completely uprooted himself, leaving all his friends and the familiar surroundings of Cardiff, and went to live with his mother in Huntly near Aberdeen. He later enrolled on a postgraduate course at Aberdeen University and bought his own flat in a village outside Aberdeen.

It was while he was sitting in a crowded lecture theatre in his first week at Aberdeen University that panic unexpectedly returned. After this first panic attack he became constantly anxious and fearful of more panic attacks and over a period of time he found that even the most simple of tasks became difficult through fear. He dropped out of university and his life became more restricted until it reached the crisis point when he was admitted to hospital.

WORKING OUT THE LINKS

In the session at this point we tried to work out if there was any link between the two main panic attacks he had described at the ages of thirteen and twenty-five. At first any link escaped Ralph, but by listing the similarities between the two situations he began to see that on both occasions he had been living by himself, isolated from his usual friends and family. In fact, throughout his life he very rarely lived anywhere by himself but always had others near him. This was something of a revelation to him. Whereas before he thought these 'terror attacks' were merely random outbursts of his hereditary 'madness', now he began to see that there might be some meaning or cause to them. At the end of our (long) first session I gave him some earlier drafts of Chapters 4 to 8 of this book to take away and read, and we arranged the next session for one week's time. He decided at the end of the session that he would go back to live with his mother instead of living by himself in his cottage.

Session 2: Ralph's fears in detail

Ralph reported the next week that he had been slightly relieved since going home to live with his mother, and although still in a state of constant tension had not been having panic attacks. He said that he was now aware through reading the chapters that panic attacks would not cause him any harm. He felt on reflection that he had been in a state of constant tension or mild panic before, but had developed ways to avoid having a full-blown panic attack.

Most of our second session was taken up in trying to understand his feelings a little more.

He described his symptoms as the need to go to the lavatory, a quickening of his pulse, palpitations, extreme tension in the forehead, cold hands, shaking, all of which happened at the same time. Typical triggers were being alone in crowded shopping areas or pubs, in queues and being alone driving the car.

His ultimate fears were that he believed that in a full-blown panic the tension would cause the chemical balance in his mind to alter his personality. He described the 'powers of reasoning' as being 'finely balanced', and an overload of anxiety might 'make it go'. He also thought the 'overload' of anxiety would make him dizzy and tense, and eventually make him urinate and pass out. He summarized this as a fear of 'losing control of the mind and body'.

His safety routines were:

▶ avoiding crowded situations

▶ being able to leave the pub at any time

▶ withdrawing from any stressful situations

▶ when going to the hairdresser, picking a particularly good moment or having a drink beforehand

▶ when in a library, concentrating on the books to stop thinking about fear

▶ avoiding picking up cups when other people were present

▶ when having to write on a blackboard having a drink beforehand

▶ trying to exhaust himself physically before attempting things

▶ cutting down on tea

▶ finding a public lavatory every so often to check his underwear to see if he had urinated in it.

His life-savers were:

▶ on a particular day when he thought he would have a panic attack he took a change of clothes with him (for fear of urination)

▶ when shaking he would try to keep himself perfectly still.

▶ He would tell himself, 'When I finally go crazy I won't know it any more and that will be OK.'

▶ he would mentally resign himself to a life of disability.

I explained to him that by carrying out these routines he never really allowed himself to discover what would actually happen during a panic attack. He would always continue to believe that 'anxiety overload' could lead to him losing control of his mind and body because the 'safety routines' he employed stopped panic attacks occurring, and even if they did start to occur he had life-saving routines to reduce them, so he constantly shielded himself from knowing what would really happen. I explained that he needed to go into the sort of situations that might set off a panic attack without 'withdrawing', as he put it.

Session 3: The 'crunch point'

Ralph returned one week later. He was still living with his mother and did not feel as isolated as before. He was also sleeping better. He had been holding on to the idea that panic attacks came down of their own accord, as I had explained in the previous session. He had tried in a limited way to test this out by going into supermarkets for a short time.

Session 3 was to be our first real-life 'exposure session'. We would carry out exercises in town rather than spending the session in the office. I explained to Ralph again that it was important for him to try to set off a panic attack and 'sweat it out' without withdrawing, so that he could discover what really happened. We had already established that large stores were most likely to set off a panic attack, so I suggested to Ralph that we should go into Aberdeen City Centre to a large store. Like most clients, this was the 'crunch point' he most feared, but I think Ralph appreciated that he couldn't move forward much more without attempting this hurdle.

So we both set off in my car to the city centre, where we parked and walked down to Debenhams. In Aberdeen, Debenhams is in a covered mall and has three storeys. We started at the bottom floor; perfumes, jewellery, men's clothes and sportswear. Although Ralph felt fear and dread, he was interested in the men's clothing section—panic had for the last two years reduced his shopping to clothes you could buy in the village shop, or what relatives happened to buy for him. As we walked round together a short wave of panic hit him but soon passed.

I must seem like a pest at times like this to clients because I am always saying, 'Did the attack pass off of its own accord or did you do something to bring it down?' exposing the little tricks and life-savers that clients are using to try to stifle a full panic attack. Well, yes, he was holding himself tense to avoid a panic attack getting worse. I again explained how he must allow the panic to come without trying to stop it in any way.

We next went up the escalator to the second floor. Again we strolled round together but as most of it was women's clothing we decided to progress to the top floor. I asked Ralph to stroll around this floor by himself and we agreed to meet at the top of the escalator five minutes later. When we met up he explained that he had had a small peak of panic at first, but this had subsided. I then asked him to spend a further twenty minutes by himself on this floor before we met up again. He achieved this satisfactorily—he had felt tension most of this time but no panic. We then went back into Debenhams self-service café for a coffee, to review what he had achieved in this session and to help plan out 'exercises' that he might carry out by himself before the next session. This may sound a pleasant end to the session, but going into a café had its own dreads, such as queuing and being trapped by having to sit at a table and finish your drink or meal. We were both very pleased with Ralph's achievements. His self-confidence was higher and, as I was to discover in the next session, he was already beginning to plan his own campaign on panic.

Session 4: Progress!

Ralph returned a week later. He had gone into a supermarket himself and had a full-blown panic attack that reached its natural peak, then declined. During this he said he was unaware of his surroundings and felt exhausted and defeated afterwards. He had expected a revelation but just felt defeat. However, over the next few days he had put his experience in perspective.

Later he pushed himself to do the week's shopping, again in the supermarket. He refused to leave the supermarket until he had got all the items on his shopping list, which in effect 'trapped him' for a period of twenty minutes or so.

He had gone to a football match in Elgin and felt awful during the first half but OK in the second (Elgin United 4: Huntly Football Club 1). He had also driven in forty miles by himself (for the first time) for our session in Aberdeen that day. Previously he had thought that forcing himself to have a panic attack would be some sort of magic drug, but he now saw that this was an over-exaggerated view and that overcoming panic would take time and persistence.

In this session we reviewed these exercises he had described and his reactions to them, and made further plans. For me what Ralph had attempted in one week showed extreme bravery!

Session 5: Come on, panic: let's get it over with!

Another week went by, and when Ralph returned for this session his list of successes included going to the supermarket, to the library, to a football match, to a huge shopping centre in Dundee, and spending three hours in a crowded restaurant.

He had stayed in these places until panic feelings had declined before leaving. He was now feeling much more positive and more willing to try things. On good days now he felt calm throughout the day with only an occasional twinge of panic.

His worst test had been in the local library where he felt a strong panic attack coming on; he said to himself, 'Come on; let's get it over with.' He felt that now the best exercises were the hardest ones—they helped to confirm to him that the problem was on the way out. He felt that the therapy was helping him not to look inwards.

BEING ALONE

Ralph was beginning to think that he would almost have to reintroduce himself to society. He had noticed that panic attacks were most likely when he went into a new environment or had to do things alone without support.

At this point we spent quite a time discussing what 'being alone' meant to Ralph. What happened in the session was that we were going back to discovering causes (as discussed in Chapters 9 and 10) rather than focusing on practical exercises to overcome his fear of panic.

To Ralph 'being alone' signified being unloved. He explained that before he was thirteen, supplies of love were a bit thin in his family. His mother had not *shown* him much affection and he had always felt a little detached from his parents. When his parents were discussing sending him to boarding school he had said to them that he would rather be with them and their friends and have a poorer education. 'But I always got the impression that they weren't listening.'

At school, when he was alone he had felt that his parents couldn't love him if they did this to him and that 'if *they* didn't love me I would never know real love in my life and never be able to sustain a relationship'.

Sessions 6 to 8: Now that panic has gone . . .

The first five sessions could be described as 'core therapy' sessions. From then on the sessions took a slightly different form. They now consisted of:

▶ reviewing practical tasks that Ralph had carried out by himself and deciding what the next steps should be

▶ reminding him of certain basic principles such as cutting out safety routines, the normality of good and bad days and the normality of fear sensations

▶ discussing in greater detail the causes for this panic, both in terms of events and in his own attitudes and approach

▶ general discussions about his tendency to be pessimistic and negative. His thoughts included, 'If I don't feel better after this therapy, I am never going to rid myself of this condition,' and 'I am dependent on the sessions. When they go I won't be able to rid myself of negative thoughts.'

▶ discussion on whether he really was a normal person or whether he had some mental weakness

▶ more discussion on the significance of being alone, 'being alienated' and the need for security

▶ discussion about his feelings of self-worth. This connected with being alone. At the back of his mind he had thought, 'When I am alone I am unloved. If I am unloved it is because I am unlovable. Therefore I am not a very nice person.'

By Session 8 he no longer believed he would lose control and was not experiencing much anxiety in places that had previously bothered him. He said he felt he had previously spent so much time being afraid of what was going on in his own body that he had not learned how to deal with external fears. He also pinpointed the fact that fear had loomed so large in his life that other feelings had been shut off or stunted and he needed more time for his emotional life to grow. He needed to develop 'emotional strength'.

The significant breakthrough was that he had decided the time was right to go back to his cottage and live alone. He did this gradually from this session onwards.

Session 9: Going back to the scene of the crime

Ralph explained how difficult it had been for him to go back to 'the place where I thought I was going crazy'. There were so many associations with the temptation to think 'I'm going crazy' and, for instance, throw himself out of the window. But, he said, 'I hold on to the idea it's not craziness, just anxiety.'

Sessions 10 to 12: Can fears be forgotten?

By Session 10 Ralph was coping quite well with living at home and by Session 11 had 'almost forgotten' about being anxious in crowded shopping areas. He did experience some tension or anxiety in certain situations and had good days and bad days, but by and large was reasonably calm. These last few sessions were taken up with discussing his life in general, how he could handle relationships better, where he was going in life and what sort of job he might aim for. Previously he had not shared feelings much with others, for instance his parents or teachers at school. Now he said that his relationship with his mother had improved a lot, that he was able to share some of his difficulties and problems with her, and to his surprise she had listened and was understanding.

Session 13: Cutting the last thread

In this our last session Ralph said that 'It [panic] has almost entirely disappeared.' He sometimes woke in the night thinking, 'Where am I going in life?' But he had decided just to leave things to fate and see how they worked out for him. 'I am not worrying about the future,' he stated. One of the last things Ralph explained to me in this session was that he felt he should cut the threads with me—our sessions were a source of security for him, and he thought that now was the time to branch out by himself. Though it is sad to say goodbye to a client, this showed me how strong and healthy Ralph's attitude to life had now become.

15

Setting Up Your Own Personal Experiment

Let's go through setting up a series of personal experiments in more detail; the nuts and bolts of facing fear. Here are some steps that panic sufferers could follow to test out what really happens in a panic:

▶ Make a list of the main situations or events that are most difficult or tend to make them panic. The list might look like this:
1   Crowds, especially in big stores
2   Queuing
3   Being in a store and not being able to see the exit
4   Sitting relaxing in the evening
5   Running up the stairs

▶ List the 'safety routines' for each of these events, in other words what they do to stop panic happening. For example:

1   CROWDS
Take a valium before I go out.
Take a friend with me.
Avoid big stores—go to smaller shops.
Go during weekdays when the crowds are less.
Only decide to go on the spur of the moment.
Only go on good days.

2 QUEUING

Don't use supermarkets.
Pick the smallest queue.
Only buy a few items of shopping.

3 BEING IN A STORE WITHOUT SEEING THE EXIT

Always make sure I know where the exit is before I go in.
Avoid stores where I might get 'trapped'.
Stay near the exit.
Make sure I can always see the exit.
Make sure I can always see my friend/partner.

4 SITTING RELAXING IN THE EVENING

Always keep busy.
Try to keep my mind active with other things to distract me.
Don't watch the TV for too long.
Always keep myself tense.
Don't watch exciting programmes, violence or topics about mental disorder.

5 RUNNING UP THE STAIRS

Never exert myself too quickly.
Creep up the stairs.
Arrange not to go upstairs too often.

▶ List the 'life-savers', in other words all those things they do once a panic starts to bring it down, such as:

Taking a deep breath
Trying to relax
Telling myself 'you'll be OK, you'll be OK'
Taking a tablet
Trying to find a chair to sit down on
Lying down on the bed
Finding a wall to lean against
Starting to run
Slapping myself
Shaking my head from side to side

Calling the doctor or a trusted friend
Drinking water
Drinking alcohol
Trying to distract myself by reading or doing mental arithmetic.

The person must:

▶ go into feared situations, such as crowds

▶ without safety routines, such as taking valium and

▶ without life-savers, such as taking a deep breath.

Sufferers would probably find it helpful to keep a written record or diary of what they achieved and what happened to them. This may include using a score system for anxiety feelings along a sliding scale (Table 4):

Table 4: A sliding scale to measure anxiety

perfectly relaxed	a bit tense		quite worked up		unpleasantly tense		very tense and panicky	terror and panic
0	1	2	3	4	5	6	7	8	9	10

Every time sufferers try a new activity they give it a score which they can record in a book or diary. This way they know whether anxiety sensations are improving or not.

One step after another

Some people are prepared to 'get stuck in' and face their worst fear straight away, once they understand how important it is. Others are more cautious. They may need to have a friend or relative with them for support at first. If so, make sure the friend reads the book so that they have an understanding of panic. Usually there are a whole series of experiments that the person needs to carry out.

Based on the example above, the sufferer might want to test something more manageable at first, like sitting relaxing in the evening. As the first experiment they might plan to sit watching TV for an hour without distracting themselves, jumping up and keeping busy doing other things. At this stage they might feel they need to choose a 'safe' programme (not violent or about mental illness). In future experiments they may wish to choose a difficult programme or just watch TV without knowing what will be shown.

WHAT WOULD A SUFFERER FIND OUT AFTER THIS FIRST EXPERIMENT?

Did they panic? If they did, were they able to see it through to the end? What did they learn? What remains to be tested out?

For their second experiment they may decide to do exactly the same thing again. They may have felt that the results were a fluke and need to find out if the same happens again. After this experiment their confidence may be rising, and they may want to make the experiment a bit more risky. They may purposely pick a violent film and plan to see it through to the end (I'm talking about the usual police films or cowboy stuff, not heavy violence).

After this they may feel that they can cope with panic at home, but are less certain about what might happen outside. They still need to carry out many mini-experiments with watching TV (for example, in the afternoon, in the late evening, by themselves, in a group, different sorts of film) and consolidate on those first experiments. But the next key experiments should be outside the home. They may try supermarkets, and later queuing in supermarkets. Later still they may try doing this on bad days. Throughout the experiments they will probably realize the extent to which they had previously tried to 'cushion' themselves from a panic, and hopefully they will begin to drop all their attempts at suppressing and controlling panic. Usually, as in Ralph's case, a person needs to carry out a whole series of personal experiments to test out the many details of their fears.

Four key principles for a sound programme of experiments

THE MAIN OBJECT OF THE EXPERIMENTS IS TO HAVE A PANIC ATTACK

If sufferers go through the experiments without ever panicking, what have they learnt? They may have learnt something useful—that panic is less frequent than they thought—and it may encourage them a lot. But there is a hidden snare. Very quietly and automatically the goal of therapy begins to change and when they finally do panic they feel devastated and deflated. All that has gone wrong is they have defined success as 'no panic' whereas the real success is having and facing a panic. If someone goes through therapy without a panic all may be well for the future; but the likelihood is that at some time in the future they will have a panic or mini-panic and be unable to deal with it. Learning about panic first-hand is the best immunization programme for the future.

FACING THE THING A PERSON FEARS MOST WILL BE UNPLEASANT, EVEN TERRIFYING

The sufferer will experience great discomfort, anxiety and fear. It takes a lot of courage. When they are changing their usual routine and facing the monster of fear they will often get worse at first, more agitated and exhausted. This is to be expected because they are pushing themselves rather than running from fear. But after this period of strain—if they are able to face their very worst fear—they will discover that there is no reality behind the fear and they will be on their way to recovery. In other words, with this approach the person can expect to get worse before getting better. The experience might be labelled 'unpleasant but safe'.

EACH EXPERIMENT MUST BE GIVEN ENOUGH TIME

A few minutes watching TV or being in crowds will not usually teach sufferers much about panic. They must continue the experiment until they feel they have discovered what they had intended to discover. Forty-five minutes is a good yardstick to have in mind for any exercise. Sometimes having to stay for a fixed amount of time means that they are 'trapped' enough to set off panic, whereas being able to escape from difficult situations at any time may be enough to stop a panic attack ever happening. So a fixed time is usually a good idea. It's amazing how something terrifying can lose its power with sufficient time. Sometimes the real power of the fear slips away without the person knowing the exact time of its departure. Some previously feared activities actually become boring after a while.

Sufferers should never attempt to leave a situation when anxiety is high or mounting—this may make the problem worse. They should try to leave after anxiety has got over the peak or when anxiety is not very high.

CHOOSING THE NEXT PERSONAL EXPERIMENT

After each experiment the person should ask, 'What do I still need to do to convince myself that panic is safe?' or, 'Deep down, what do I still feel is dangerous about having a panic attack?' The answers can be used to guide future experiments. It is quite common for people to carry out their personal experiments on good days. What do they learn? They learn they can cope on good days, but they still feel very uneasy about doing tasks on bad days. Would something awful happen on those days when dread and depression are so close at hand? This is the clue for the next experiment—purposely doing the same tasks on bad days. If the person can discover that even then panic is safe, this really helps to dismantle bad days. They occur less.

Different people vary in the pace they can take the experiments—one person, like Terry, may do the most risky experiment first whereas others prefer to increase the risk factor only little by little. That's OK if they are learning something new about panic each time.

PART V

The Panic Sufferer as Normal

16

Cures, Half-Cures and Limitations

Why should someone go through all the pain and anxiety of these personal experiments? To be worthwhile the sufferer has to press in on those very things they are most afraid of—and that is agonizing at times. But is it worth it?

Why bother?

These are the typical benefits of the therapy:

▶ panic attacks will occur less often

▶ panic attacks will be far less severe

▶ even if the odd panic occurs in the future the person will feel uncomfortable but not afraid

▶ the person will feel more relaxed, and does not have to fight off impending panics or struggle to control panic

▶ the amazing clutter of avoidance behaviour, safety routines and life-savers will start to disappear

▶ the person's mood will lift. They will feel less generally anxious, depressed and feel less dread.

▶ the person will not need to depend on tranquillizers or take anti-depressants

▶ the person will be able to get on with their life and personal development rather than be locked into a prison of fear (though note that recovery may affect the balance of relationships—others may have to adapt to a less dependent person)

▶ the person's social, work, sex, and leisure life should be much more free.

What if I can't face personal experiments?

This is entirely up to the discretion of an individual. Everyone is different, and what suits one may not suit another. For many individuals, simply knowing the facts about panic seems to be all they need. Others need to prove it to themselves.

It may be that the person is just too fearful to attempt any experiments or is not convinced it is necessary. In this case it may be better not to try. Some try and have to give up—they certainly shouldn't feel that is a failure.

Often people need the strong support of others to get through these experiments. Very often the guiding knowledge and support of a therapist is necessary. For them a self-help book is just not enough. What are they to do? They probably need the individual guidance and help of a clinical psychologist or nurse trained in cognitive-behavioural therapy, or they may want some medication to help them. They should go to their own doctor for advice in the first instance, and if they want to see a clinical psychologist they should ask their own doctor to refer them on to one, though often there may be a waiting time before they can be seen.

Once they are seen the psychologist will interview them in some depth and try to understand the problem in detail. They may well be able to identify why the person is not succeeding with the approach in this book and will present their own solutions for overcoming the problem. There is variation from one psychologist to another and they may well use a different approach from mine. There are also many other advantages of talking to someone face to face. Sometimes the relief in talking to someone who understands the problem is very helpful.

There are also a number of self-help groups for panic and anxiety sufferers, usually run on a voluntary basis by the sufferers themselves. They are often useful in helping the person realize that they are not alone in their suffering, and in providing support and care from those who understand.

The sufferer is the best judge of whether to attempt these exercises and there should be no sense of shame or failure for someone who doesn't want to do them. Everyone's individual circumstances are different and we are talking about a serious and powerful enemy—fear—which is not to be underestimated.

When should personal experiments not be done?

There are cases where an experiment should not be done. The obvious ones are those in which the person has a known diagnosed condition, such as a diagnosed heart condition or asthma, in which exertion or strain makes them worse. If an asthmatic does a personal experiment it may have the reverse effect—rather than showing how safe panic is, it may show how dangerous it is. The guiding principle should be: if in doubt consult your GP about what to do.

When should a person stop doing personal experiments?

The simple answer is, 'When they have discovered what they need to know about panic'. There is no need to keep experiments going for months and months. An upper limit for a series of experiments would be about four months. They are for the purpose of discovery. Once someone has discovered the facts about their panic anxiety, there's no need to keep going on and on. Certainly experiments should not become a way of life, rather, they should be one stage of life which can later be forgotten.

How far can recovery go?

A full recovery is possible. But what do we mean by 'a full recovery'? It does *not* mean that the person will be 100 per cent free of panic attacks. If 100 per cent freedom is the goal of therapy then there is a problem—it probably means that the person is still afraid of panics. With a full recovery the person is no longer afraid of panic attacks, and not thrown if they should have the occasional panic. They may experience panic and anxiety from time to time if they are going through periods of stress and difficulty. It would be normal to expect that. However, if the person is not afraid of this and realizes that they are not 'slipping back' any panicky phase should not last too long; it is unpleasant but not threatening. Over a longer period of time panics may disappear altogether.

What if I've done everything the book says and am no better?

If after carefully following the ideas in this book a sufferer is not improving they should stop 'bashing their head against a brick wall' and discontinue the exercises.

But remember:

▶ the person must really put their fear of dying, going mad or whatever it may be to the test. If they keep avoiding it, even with clever tricks, they have not really done the exercises properly—and cannot expect a full recovery.

▶ the person must continue with the approach for long enough to really find out what happens. Dipping a toe in the water just won't work. For instance if someone goes into crowds once and leaves it at that, they have not given the experiment a full enough test.

▶ if the person does all the exercises but never has a panic attack they may realize that the activities are safe enough, but they haven't discovered that panic attacks are also safe. If in the future they do happen to have a panic they will be thrown. So it is the panic attack that must be faced, not the activities or places that set off a panic.

▶ when sufferers try to set off a panic attack—let's say by going into crowds—they must stay long enough for the panic to happen and then to subside. Five minutes will not usually be enough—it's more like an hour that is needed.

▶ patience is required—the person can't expect an overnight cure. I have heard it said that it takes the same amount of time to get over a stress problem as it took to develop. I don't know about that—it certainly isn't scientifically proved—but it is right in one sense: the idea of an immediate wonder-cure is a snare to the sufferer.

▶ the person should not let a set-back make them think that the approach is failing. Set-backs are normal. There *will* be set-backs. They do *not* spell failure.

If after carrying out all this advice there is no obvious improvement, it's time to stop.

17

Let's Finish Off Panic

In this chapter I would like to draw the main points of this book together.

▶ A panic attack is the body's normal fear reaction. Everyone has the potential for a fear reaction. Usually the fear reaction is switched on when danger comes along. It is there to help us escape quickly from the danger. In the first few attacks of the panic sufferer the fear reaction was switched on *by accident*.

▶ But sufferers don't know that. They think that because the feelings of the fear reaction were so strong, something really serious must be happening to them.

▶ The fear reaction has been accidentally switched on through a time of stress, crisis or series of changes in the sufferer's life in the nine months before their first panic.

▶ Sufferers do not make the connection between their life stress and the first panic attacks.

▶ Not knowing the real cause of the panics, a sufferer becomes very afraid of more attacks and what might happen to them during the attacks.

▶ This fear changes them. They begin to become oversensitive to any feelings resembling panic, to look inwards too much, to try to find ways to stop panic happening or 'neutralize' it when it starts.

▶ The effort to avoid panic clutters up and changes the person's life. They spend far too much time and energy taking precautions and evading panic feelings.

▶ Sufferers are basically the same as they ever were but are so caught up by fear that they seem to change. However, once they understand what is happening to them and lose their fear of panic, they can get back to normal.

The contribution of this book

This book has been arranged in five sections. The first provided a basic explanation about panic. The second covered some of the typical mistaken ideas people have about panic and the third looked at how to identify causes for panic. The fourth section describes how to test out what really happens in panic by using 'personal experiments'. This is the practical back-up to the earlier chapters concerning mistaken ideas, but instead of being informed by others of the facts, the sufferer is encouraged to discover the truth through their own personal experience.

Why panic sufferers are normal

The panic sufferer does not have any mental aberrations or illness, but is a normal individual because:

▶ the first panics have a definite and logical cause (crisis/stress)

▶ the fear reaction (which is the same as a panic attack) is common to everyone

▶ the reason panics can continue over a long period of time involve the sufferer's lack of understanding about panics and mistaken ideas which cause them to avoid panic

▶ the strength of the sufferer's fear about what others may call harmless (for example, crowds or palpitations) is entirely reasonable given their mistaken ideas about panic being dangerous. They are reacting to danger just as a person should do.

The main culprit is the sufferer's mistaken idea about the danger of panic. This can be corrected by

▶ accurate information

▶ personal 'corrective' experience.

Restoring and rebuilding

Although for the sufferer panics appear completely bewildering and illogical, once they begin to understand the fear reaction it all makes sense. There is much suffering involved in panic; the panic sufferer's life revolves around panic and fear. It is possible to overcome this and return from that terrifying orbit around fear to being able to concentrate on normal everyday life, but when this happens the person will have some catching up to do. The years of concentration on panic often means that the sufferer has missed out on so many of the ordinary things in life. Fortunately their problem does not permanently damage their mental faculties which are untouched through the worst panic experience. Concentration, memory, feeling at ease—none of this is permanently lost, only temporarily suppressed by fear, and all this can return again. If you are a panic sufferer yourself, I hope it *does* return again for you.

Postscript
The Subject Matter Catches Up with the Author

A strange thing happened during the writing of this book. I had started off writing for those who suffer from panic—I had some feeling for them and an understanding of what they were going through. Despite my knowledge of their condition, I was basically writing for 'them', the sufferers . But during the course of writing this book I too became one of 'them'. For the first time in my life I experienced an anxiety and panic disturbance that took me about nine months to get over. I was reluctant to mention my own account in this book at first but decided it might help others in their struggle with panic.

The whole thing caught me unawares. Looking back I should have seen it coming. You would expect a clinical psychologist to be able to spot the warning signs in himself! But I didn't. At least, I did realize I was under stress, but assumed it would blow over and things would get back to normal again.

A night I'd rather forget
One night shortly after going to bed my physiological system seemed to go into a different gear. Instead of my body slowing down and quickly dropping off to sleep (the normal routine), everything seemed to be speeding up—heart beat, sweating, tension, faster breathing.

At first I didn't worry, simply saying to myself, 'relax—it will pass, as usual'. But after several attempts to go to sleep my whole system was still racing and getting faster, not slower. It doesn't sound so very fantastic or particularly scary as I tell it now but as my attempts to shrug it off failed I began to get concerned. I woke my wife to talk. I went downstairs to make hot milk. I tried some aspirin—but was still sweating, getting hotter, really tense. I was not able to breath properly, and my heart was racing.

I suppose one advantage of being a psychologist was that I instantly identified it as anxiety, not some physical disorder, but that didn't stop it happening. I was tossing and turning a lot, so decided to go down to the lounge to set up a makeshift bed there. After watching a bit of late-night television hoping to distract myself and after yet more hot milk I tried again to sleep. This would have been about two to three hours after the attack started. Still everything was twice as fast as normal.

Fear steps in

Somewhere around this stage, after all my efforts to calm down had failed, fear seemed to step in. Looking back now, the event is organized in my mind, and I am presenting a much clearer picture of what happened. At the time it was unclear, chaotic and very, very unpleasant. Many of the fears related to the future. They were all of a type we could call 'supposing' fears:

▶ 'Supposing' my body carried on at this rate, I could never get to sleep. I couldn't do my job properly. I would lose my job, be made redundant, not be able to support my family.

▶ 'Supposing' my body carried on at this rate, I would be continuously aware of my heartbeat and breathing and not be able to concentrate on the more detailed things one needs to do as a clinical psychologist—such as listening carefully to patients, picking up clues from what they said, working out what to focus on next in the session, giving a lecture or writing an article.

▶ 'Supposing' I was continuously aware of heartbeat and breathing I would have no peace, and be in constant misery.

Over the next few days I continued at work, though not giving of my best to patients—the feeling of dread and intrusive awareness of unpleasant bodily sensations made it quite difficult to concentrate on the sessions. I remember on the Friday there was an annual local meeting of psychologists, and I had to give a brief presentation about research. I was sweating profusely and tending to pant and sigh a lot, but tried to cover this up in the presentation. I wonder if any of my colleagues noticed my distress.

Beyond normal experience

At an early stage I recalled the comment panic sufferers often made that it was impossible for others to understand how painful the experience was for them. I could now understand what they were talking about. The general mood I experienced was one of pervasive dread and fear of staying like this, followed after a few weeks by a longer depressed period in which I lost my sense of purpose in life. I slept little over the months. It struck me once or twice that this experience was like my idea of hell. Previous experiences of 'normal' anxiety, such as exams, visiting the dentist or having to give a speech simply did not equip me in understanding what was happening now. I seemed to have entered a sort of different mood-world that was qualitatively different from anything I had experienced before.

Weathering the storm

In that first week, when I was at a low ebb, the parable that Jesus told about a wise man building his house on rock came to mind. When the wind and rains came and beat down, the house on the rock stood firm. Although I felt appalling and my emotions were about as far from 'peace' as can be imagined, surprisingly my faith in God stayed firm. I was able to pray to him (which I did more than usual!) and hear from him as well as normally. Any closeness or reality was all now, *in the present*; I had no hope for recovery in the future, no sense or promise that I would ever get out of this.

The experience was as close to a solid rock in the midst of storms as any other analogy I can think of. Something quite central in my life was remaining stable while other things were falling to pieces, and this was important to my eventual recovery.

Red-hot coals

A firm understanding of panic and anxiety symptoms was ingrained in me when my own problem started. I had regularly explained panic symptoms to patients and had spent hours reading about them and thinking about them for this book. Knowing what was happening—what the sensations were—and particularly knowing that no harm such as madness or heart attack could come of them was a tremendous benefit. It probably reduced my symptoms from the very start. This has reinforced my belief that correct understanding of panic attacks is very important. The problem did seem to seek out areas where my knowledge was a bit weak, but I did some 'revision' which eventually helped.

Technically, what I experienced was not full-blown panic attacks, but could be described as 'limited panic attacks'—only certain symptoms occurred and they did not rise to a climax like a panic attack. The problem was closer to a more continuous overawareness of bodily sensations.

I spent a great deal of time trying to reason myself out of sensations or persuade myself they were safe. An important part of recovery was to regard thoughts/awareness of bodily sensations as red-hot coals, that I had to 'drop' as soon as they came to mind rather than ruminating over them. Over the months this meant that I got less self-absorbed.

So what?

A breakthrough occurred one Sunday, after my wife and I had been for a walk with a couple who are our close friends. As we walked I tried to explain to the husband how the problem was really disrupting my life and how I felt under a cloud of moderate dread or fear so often now. Later in the afternoon, when we had returned home an idea came to me that was a bit like a 'Eureka' feeling. The idea is not so very surprising, and I'm sure I'd thought it several times before without it having any impact on me at all. But this time it really did 'click': 'If I am aware of my heart rate and breathing—*so what?*' From that point I put into operation all the exercises about facing fear described in this book. Before, I had been trying to avoid awareness of certain bodily sensations. Now I tried to increase them. I said the words 'heart-rate' aloud several times. I kept purposely thinking of the things I had previously feared and avoided. I pondered how to purposely increase these sensations, and hit on the idea of jogging. I regularly jogged from then on. I still have the sneaky feeling that after our walk my friend had been praying for me.

Plodding on

Things progressed from this point, not necessarily smoothly, but they progressed. After about eight months the point was reached where I had forgotten for most of the day that there was a problem. In my recovery, some words of the author Claire Weekes had been percolating in my mind ever since I had written a review chapter on an article she had written, called *The Key to Resisting Relapse in Panic*[26]. These words proved helpful and encouraged me to persist in adopting the right attitude whenever a set-back occurred. They were:

Memory is always capable of recalling nervous symptoms, and what a heyday an anxious inner voice has then. It says 'It's all back again! Every lock, stock and barrel. Every member of the family! We're all here. What are you going to do now? You'll never recover now, you know!' What power the wrong voice holds. But if the right learned voice is there it will come to the rescue and say, 'You've been here before, you know the way!' Then, in spite of being possibly shocked and temporarily thrown off balance, the owner of that inner voice does know what to do and gradually does it.

Have the problems disappeared? Certain bodily sensations or moods such as tension, lack of concentration, increased heart-rate do still occur when I am overworked or stressed in some way. That's only to be expected. But what is now missing is fear, fear of these feelings. And what a difference that makes.

Books and Articles Mentioned in this Book

Chapter 1

1 American Psychiatric Association (1987), *Diagnostic and Statistical Manual of Mental Disorders*, Third Edition, Revised. American Psychiatric Association, Washington, D.C.

2 McFadyen, M. (1989), 'The Cognitive Invalidation Approach to Panic', Chapter 13, in R. Baker (ed.), *Panic Disorder: Theory, Research and Therapy*, John Wiley, Chichester.

3 Kelly, G.A. (1963), *A Theory of Personality*, Norton, New York.

4 Baker, R. (ed.) (1989), *Panic Disorder: Theory, Research and Therapy*, John Wiley, Chichester.

5 Baker, R. (1989), 'Personal Accounts of Panic', Chapter 5 in R. Baker (ed.), *Panic Disorder: Theory, Research and Therapy*, John Wiley, Chichester.

6 Baker, R. (1990), *Research Interview Study on Panic Attacks*, Department of Clinical Psychology, Royal Cornhill Hospital, Grampian Health Board, Aberdeen.

7 Baker, R. and McFadyen, M. (1985), 'Cognitive Invalidation and the Enigma of Exposure', in E. Karas (ed.), *Current Issues in Clinical Psychology*, 2, Plenum Press, New York.

8 Baker, R., 'Emotional Processing and Panic'. For publication in *Behaviour Research and Therapy Journal*.

9 Baker, R., Nunn, J. and Sinclair, J. (1993), *A System for Evaluating the Effectiveness of Therapy*. Final Report of Clinical Audit Study to the Grampian Health Board, Aberdeen.

Chapter 2

10 Vose, R.H. (1981), *Agoraphobia*, Faber and Faber, London.

11 McKinnon, P. (1983), *In Stillness Conquer Fear*, Dove Communications, Blackburn, Victoria.

12 Freedman, R. (1989), 'Ambulatory Monitoring Findings on Panic', Chapter 4 in R. Baker (ed.), *Panic Disorder: Theory, Research and Therapy*, John Wiley, Chichester.

13 Zane, M. D. (1989), 'A Contextual Approach to Panic', Chapter 8 in R. Baker (ed.), *Panic Disorder: Theory, Research and Therapy*, John Wiley, Chichester.

14 Agras, W.S., Sylvester, D., and Oliveau, D.C. (1969), 'The epidemiology of common fears and phobias', *Comprehensive Psychiatry*, **10**, pp 191–97.

Chapter 3

15 Raymond, E. (1946), *The Autobiography of David*, Victor Gollanz, London.

Chapter 5

16 Basoglu, M., Marks, I.M., and Sengun, S. (1992), 'A Prospective Study of Anxiety in Agoraphobia with Panic Disorder', *British Journal of Psychiatry*, **160**, pp 57–64.

17 Kenardy, J., Fried, L., Kraemer, and Barr Taylor, C. (1992), 'Psychological Precursors of Panic Attacks', *British Journal of Psychiatry*, **160**, pp 668–73.

18 Waring, H. (1989), 'The Nature of Panic Attack Symptoms', Chapter 2 in R. Baker (ed.), *Panic Disorder: Theory, Research and Therapy*, John Wiley, Chichester.

Chapter 6

19 Kezdi, P. (1981), *You and Your Heart: How to take care of your heart for a long healthy life,* Penguin, Harmondsworth.

20 Weekes, C. (1972), *Peace from Nervous Suffering*, Angus and Robertson, London.

21 Van Den Hout, M., De Jong, P., and Merchelbach, H. (1993), 'On the termination of panic attacks', *Behaviour Research and Therapy*, **31,**, pp 117–18.

Chapter 9

22 Clark, J.C. and Wardman, W. (1985), *Agoraphobia: A Clinical and Personal Account*, Pergamon, Sydney.

23 Hibbert, G.A. (1984), 'Ideational components of anxiety: their origin and content', *British Journal of Psychiatry*,**144**, pp 618–24.

Chapter 11

24 Mathews, A.M., Gelder, M.G. and Johnston, D.W. (1981), *Agoraphobia: Nature and Treatment*, Tavistock Publications, London.

Chapter 12

25 Spielberger, C.D. (1972), 'Anxiety as an Emotional State', in C.D. Spielberger (ed.), *Anxiety: Current Trends in Theory and Research*, **Vol. 1**, Academic Press, New York.

Postscript

26 Weekes, C. and Baker, R. (1989), 'The Key to Resisting Relapse in Panic', Chapter 15 in R. Baker (ed.), *Panic Disorder: Theory, Research and Therapy*, John Wiley, Chichester.

General Recommended Reading for Panic and Agoraphobia

For sufferers:

Weekes, C. (1962), *Self-Help for your Nerves*, Angus and Robertson, London.

Weekes, C. (1972), *Peace from Nervous Suffering*, Angus and Robertson, London.

Weekes, C. (1984), *More Help for your Nerves*, Angus and Robertson, London.

Marks, I.M. (1978), *Living with Fear*, McGraw-Hill, New York.

For therapists:

Barlow, D.H. and Cerny, J.A. (1988), *Psychological Treatment of Panic*, The Guilford Press, Treatment Manuals for Practitioners, New York.

McFadyen, M. (1989), 'The Cognitive Invalidation Approach to Panic', Chapter 13 in R. Baker (ed.), *Panic Disorder: Theory, Research and Therapy*, John Wiley, Chichester.

Index

Also from Lion Publishing:

CLIMBING OUT OF DEPRESSION

Sue Atkinson

Depression is a dark and isolating experience. Countless people suffer from it.

Anyone who has fallen into a pit of depression wants to climb back out. But that is not easy to do. Depressed people often feel paralyzed into inaction.

So help is needed—practical, humane and spiritual help— which is just what this book offers.

Sue Atkinson has suffered years of depression herself. She does not write as an expert on depression, or a depression counsellor, but as someone who knows the feelings from close personal experience.

This is a book to dip into as fits a person's mood and the need of the moment. The reader will find it a dependable guide for the climb.

ISBN 0 7459 2248 1